GEEK
WISDOM

THE
SACRED TEACHINGS
OF
NERD CULTURE

EDITED BY STEPHEN H. SEGAL

With commentary by Zaki Hasan, N. K. Jemisin,

Eric San Juan, and Genevieve Valentine

ILLUSTRATIONS BY MARIO ZUCCA

QUIRK BOOKS
PHILADELPHIA

Library of Congress Cataloging-in-Publication Number: 2011922702
ISBN: 978-1-59474-527-0

Printed in China

Typeset in Futura and Bembo
Designed by Doogie Horner and Steven DeCusatis
Illustrations by Mario Zucca
Production management by John J. McGurk

Quirk Books
215 Church Street
Philadelphia, PA 19106
quirkbooks.com

10 9 8

DEDICATION

This book is dedicated to everyone who's ever said one of these things out loud during conversation.

(Especially John, Greg, Mike, Lori, Jeannie, Chris, Ben, Paul, Steve, Paul, Nina, Lisa, Jenn, Cameron, Tempest, Vanessa, Julie, and Stu. I have been, and always shall be, et cetera, et cetera.)

TABLE OF
CONTENTS

INTRODUCTION

I wish I could remember who asked me the question. Because I know for sure that my answer is what set me on the path that has brought me here, to you, on this page. The question was: "What was your religion when you were growing up?" And my answer was: "Uh, science fiction, pretty much."

I meant it as a joke. I was poking fun at myself, saying that I'd been such a freaking *geek* as a kid, watching *Star Trek* and reading Tolkien and writing computer programs and building TARDIS models, you'd think that stuff was my religion. But as soon as it came out of my mouth, I immediately understood that this was no joke. It was absolutely 100 percent true in a way that I'd never thought of before—and, furthermore, it was a good thing.

What *is* religion? Never mind all the trappings, all the ceremonial garments and the prayer rules and the fish on Friday. What is religion really for? It's a framework of ideas—a body of thought shared by a community, written and handed down through literature—that's intended to guide us toward maturity by helping us ask and answer the big, cosmic questions about existence. Who are we? Where did we come from? Is there anyone else out there in realms of being we can't see? Here on earth, why can't we get along with one another better than we do? And how can we possibly find any redemption for the mess we tend to make of things?

The Bible tells stories answering these questions. So does the Quran. So do the Upanishads. So do the sacred books of every other religion. The stories in each tradition vary a lot in the details, but they all make their way around to more or less the same points that, in turn, ultimately boil down to this: Hey, show some respect for the universe, because it's a whole lot bigger than you.

You know what? Religion isn't the only place to find those kinds of stories. The modern scientific world tells them, too. In fact, geek culture is built on them.

Look at the Bible. In the beginning, God gave Adam and Eve a couple simple rules, and they didn't obey them, and we got to see how that affected the rest of their lives and what it implies for us. Then Moses brought down ten divine algorithms from the Mount for everyone to live by—don't kill, don't bear false witness, do honor your parents, etc.—and we got to spend the rest of the Bible tagging along as generations upon generations of slaves, peasants, merchants, and kings alternately followed and broke these commandments and tried to learn how to live with the consequences.

And now look at Isaac Asimov, scientist and novelist. He was not, obviously, God. He didn't create the universe, humanity, and everything in between. But he did imagine that someday humanity would create artificial beings—mechanical intelligences—and would have to give *them* rules to live by. And thus, after school, while my best friend John was in catechism class reading from the Gospel of Matthew, I could be found at home reading from Asimov's book *I, Robot*, watching cybernetic Abrahams and Jobs with "names" like SPD-1 and NS-10 do their damnedest to make it through situations where the rules of life seemed just impossible to cope with.

Does that sound strange? That robots, as envisioned as realistically as possible by a scientifically trained futurist, should suffer from existential angst? In fact, it makes tremendous sense. Because when Asimov sat down to codify his Laws of Robotics— the practical operational rules that would make it possible for these new intelligent beings to live in harmony with one another and their creators—what he came up with was startlingly similar to the moral code outlined by most every religion and philosophy throughout human history. Oh, sure, it looks different—

1. A robot shall not harm a human being or, through inaction, allow a human being to come to harm.

2. A robot shall obey the orders given by a human being, except where this would conflict with the First Law.

3. A robot shall protect its own existence, except where this would conflict with the First or Second Law.

—but when you put that in plainer, more casual language, what it amounts to is this:

It's important to take care of yourself, but it's more important to spread happiness, but it's even more important to hold life sacred.

You don't have to be a robot, or even a sci-fi geek, to understand that's a pretty straightforward description of being a good person. And, you know, being a good person is hard. So if geek culture can offer fresh, new, alternative paths to all the eternal truths that religion and philosophy have managed to discover over the past few thousand years—paths that welcome those who've been turned away from the more traditional routes—then I say, let there be geekery.

The realm of geekdom, of course, is much bigger than just science fiction. Geeks are passionate fans of stuff, and particularly of stuff that lies somewhere along one of two cultural axes: *math* and *myth*. The love of math stuff gives us science geeks, computer geeks, chess geeks; the love of myth stuff gives us theater geeks, literary geeks, ancient-Greek geeks. This is why science fiction and role-playing games make up the enduring popular image of modern-day geekdom, mind you, because those are the places where math and myth intersect: literature built on the infinite possibilities of science, improv sword and sorcery shaped by the numerical output of 20-sided dice.

Hence *Geek Wisdom*: the first compendium of sacred teachings from the wide-ranging "holy scriptures" of geekdom, that weird mass of pop culture and high art ranging from blockbuster movies to esoteric novels to cult-classic T-shirt slogans. *Star Wars*. *The Princess Bride*. Albert Einstein. Stan Lee. From such sources we've gathered (and mused thoughtfully upon) the deepest, purest, most profound ideas and sayings to be found. The ones that cut right to the heart of life in the twenty-first century. The ones we quote as if they'd come from the Bible, or from Shakespeare. The ones that, increasingly, have emerged from the underground to form the cellular structure of a true new culture canon.

Our culture canon. And thus does the geek inherit the earth.

A NOTE ON SPOILERS

GEEK WISDOM features quotes from many classic movies, books, and television shows. Some of the points we necessarily address will, technically, be spoilers to anyone who hasn't experienced these works directly. We have avoided, however, ruining any big surprises or twist endings; the spoilers found within are the kind of thing you'd pick up from general cultural discussion of the stories in question. In other words: A few bits may be *spoiled*, but don't worry—none of them are *ruined*.

I.
MY NAME IS
INIGO MONTOYA

(WISDOM ABOUT THE SELF)

"WITH GREAT POWER COMES GREAT RESPONSIBILITY."

—STAN LEE, MARVEL COMICS

SPIDER-MAN'S UNCLE told him this, and that's why he became Spider-Man. George Washington realized it, too, and that's why he decided eight years was long enough for anyone to be president of the United States. Tim Allen tried to dodge around it, and that's why his dishwasher exploded. King David said to hell with it and had his lover's husband killed, and that's why he had epic family problems for the rest of his life. Paris Hilton seems oblivious to the very concept, and that's why animal lovers have long been inclined to worry about her poor, poor dog. And Albert Einstein realized the full, inhuman horror of it—that's why he wrote to Franklin Roosevelt to explain the possibility of an atomic bomb. Sure, the seed of the truism can be found in Luke 12:48 ("To whom much is given, much is expected"). But although the word of that uppity young Jewish carpenter from Nazareth may be eternal, it took an uppity young Jewish comic-book writer from New York City to put it in terms that ring true to the modern ear.

The original quote, from *Amazing Fantasy* #15 (1962), actually said: "With great power there must also come—great responsibility!" Subsequent references rounded off the portentous edges.

"DESTINY! DESTINY! NO ESCAPING THAT FOR ME!"

—DR. FREDERICK FRANKENSTEIN, *YOUNG FRANKENSTEIN*

THE ODDS ARE EXCELLENT that your grandfather did not dig up corpses, stitch them together, and reanimate them into a murderous, shambling monstrosity. And yet the same inexorable force of genetic history that drove young Frederick to follow in Victor's footsteps is at work in all our lives. Maybe you realize one day, washing your hands for the fourth time since dinner, that somewhere along the line you picked up the same obsessive germaphobia that always made your mom's aunt seem so crazy. Maybe you've just chosen between three different neighborhoods to live in, and you can't figure out *why* you picked the one with the longest commute, until it finally hits your conscious mind that standing outside your new window is a willow tree like the one Dad planted in your backyard when you were nine. Maybe, after a lifetime of gorgeous hair, you're staring down the barrel of a .22-caliber bald head. Whatever it may look like, there is definitely a monster with your family's name—and it's coming for you. It's up to you whether you'll chase it with a burning torch or sing it a sweet lullaby of love.

Filmmaker Mel Brooks has called *Young Frankenstein* (1974) his favorite of all his movies.

"I'M NOT FINISHED."

—EDWARD, *EDWARD SCISSORHANDS*

IT'S HARD FOR ANY SENSITIVE adolescent to have a reasoned, distanced approach to *Edward Scissorhands*. That's because it's one of film's most heartbreaking portrayals of the experience of being a teenage outsider. The horrors of suburban conformity are distilled to their pure essence in the people who surround Edward, all of whom are pretty shells over darker selves. The movie makes several salient points about how this microcosm behaves toward someone who's physically different; even Edward's adoptive mother, who loves him dearly, often treats him more as a cause célèbre than as a person. And even after he finds someone to love, he has to leave her to avoid retribution from those who don't understand him. When Edward whispers, "I'm not finished"—referring to his very self, that is, "My creator didn't give me all the necessary bits"—it's as though he's speaking directly to every uncertain kid who ever longed to be accepted without having to conform. Luckily, growing up "unfinished" can make geeks the very best people to guide and nurture the next generation of outsiders: We know you don't have to be finished to be awesome.

Goth-geek favorite filmmaker Tim Burton is a master of moody visuals first and a narrative storyteller only second. But he has called *Edward Scissorhands* (1990) semiautobiographical, which may explain why the plot is among Burton's strongest.

"THE LIGHT THAT BURNS TWICE AS BRIGHT BURNS HALF AS LONG . . . AND YOU HAVE BURNED SO VERY, VERY BRIGHTLY, ROY."

—DR. ELDON TYRELL, *BLADE RUNNER*

D R. TYRELL WASN'T TALKING about rock and roll, but he might as well have been. See, when Neil Young told us it was better to burn out than to fade away, he wasn't being sincere; his own status as the elder statesmen of grungy rock is proof of that. He was talking about an all-too-common phenomenon, though: Often, our most monumental cultural icons, in music or otherwise, are monumental in part because they were taken from us too soon. Whether through their own recklessness (Jimi Hendrix, Jim Morrison), by their own hand (Kurt Cobain, Ernest Hemingway), or at the hands of another (John Lennon, Abraham Lincoln), the life lived in the clouds above mere mortals is frequently doomed to the fate of Icarus, who flew too close to the sun and in his folly perished. *Is* it better for a superstar's legacy if, like *Blade Runner*'s wild-eyed Roy Batty, they burn out rather than fade away? Or should the next wave of ambitious, creative visionaries buck this trend and stick around for their own third acts? The geek takeover of popular culture just may mean a shift in this unfortunate tradition; unlike rockers and replicants, one thing geeks are *not* is reckless.

After decades of proudly gleaming Hollywood spaceships and robots, *Blade Runner* (1982) offered an alternate version of the future, full of grimy streets and corporate advertising. It's a future that's looked more like the present every year since.

"BY GRABTHAR'S HAMMER, BY THE SONS OF WARVAN, YOU SHALL BE AVENGED."

—ALEXANDER DANE, *GALAXY QUEST*

SOMETIMES IT'S HARD to accept one's inner weirdo. In *Galaxy Quest*, jaded actor Alexander Dane finds his thespian career ruined by sci-fi typecasting, and thus spends most of the movie trying to distance himself from his TV character's most famous catchphrase. In the end, though, he learns that some situations call for those very words to be wielded sincerely, in the name of justice. It's not hard to find oneself in this position. The world is frequently cruel to those earnest souls who take "corny" ideas like truth and justice seriously or aren't afraid to wear their hearts on their sleeves—just look at how often the wondrous power of the Internet is used for callous, drive-by snark when commiseration is really what's called for. Folks are eager to point and laugh at the latest online meme making the rounds. After we saw a photo of Keanu Reeves looking genuinely sad get Photoshopped into a thousand comedic punch lines, it was only to be expected that the video clip of that random dude getting excited about a double rainbow was going to be mocked a millionfold. Yet expressing oneself passionately is nothing to be ashamed of. It's a way to clearly communicate the things that, deep down, are most important to us. In fact, *someone* had better do it, or, by Grabthar's Hammer, who shall bother avenging you?

Sometimes, parody or pastiche shows a deeper love for the original source material than a hundred official sequels ever could. In forty years, has there really ever been a better *Star Trek* movie than *Galaxy Quest* (1999)—or a better *Fantastic Four* movie than *The Incredibles*?

"ALL THAT IS GOLD DOES NOT GLITTER / NOT ALL THOSE WHO WANDER ARE LOST."

—J. R. R. TOLKIEN, *THE LORD OF THE RINGS: THE FELLOWSHIP OF THE RING*

TOLKIEN may have been able to more easily sum up his verse description of Aragorn by saying, "Don't judge a book by its cover," but that wouldn't have been very poetic, would it? Like his belief in huge and unexpected good fortune—he coined the term *eucatastrophe* to describe such sudden turns for the good—Tolkien believed in finding virtue in unexpected places, often wrapped in a cloak the modern world would deems ugly. Gnarled tree creatures, road-weary travelers, and grumpy old men in grey rags are just a few of the guises taken by the benevolent powers of Middle Earth. There may be a degree of simple wish-fulfillment fantasy hidden in there, the old cliché of the ordinary person who secretly has amazing abilities, but it's more than that. It's a lesson in judging people—or, rather, *not* judging them. It also speaks to appreciating simplicity in one's life and not underestimating the inner strength of the downtrodden. Despite Tolkien's staunch Catholicism, there is an almost Taoist spirit to the sentiment. Divinity is not labeled as such; you have to look below the surface.

We finally met Aragorn onscreen forty-seven years after his literary debut in 1954; few could fault Viggo Mortensen's performance as the exiled heir to humankind's throne, but some did grumble that, even scruffy, he was more handsome than Aragorn's epigraph should allow.

"I'M NOT EVEN SUPPOSED TO BE HERE TODAY!"

—DANTE HICKS, *CLERKS*

JUST READING that makes you want to slap someone, doesn't it? And yet, at the same time, you totally get it, don't you? Most of us are well acquainted with the sting of being abruptly summoned to spend our off-day working; still, it's not pretty when on-the-job complaints turn into life-sweeping disclaimers. Whiny retail employee Dante Hicks drops this gem approximately eight hundred (thousand) times in this classic slice-of-slacker-life film; specifically, he seems to drop it whenever he's made an error of judgment, as if uttering the words will both send him home and erase his mistakes. Unfortunately, suffering injustice doesn't excuse you from responsibility for your own choices, and Dante spends the day forcibly coming to terms with this fact—or, at least, being dressed down about it by Randal. (Please note that we recommend taking stock of your choices and trying to get closure, instead of just arguing about whether contractors on the Death Star were innocent victims or not.) But don't worry—as long as you're not using it as a catch-all excuse, if you're called in to work on your day off, you're totally still allowed to complain.

It's rarely commented on, since the name Dante experienced a trendy baby boom a couple decades ago, but we do think the idea of naming the protagonist of *Clerks* (1994) after the poet who famously toured all the torments of Hell is a pretty funny bit of hyperbole.

"WAX ON . . . WAX OFF."

—MR. MIYAGI, *THE KARATE KID*

N O ONE ENJOYS ROTE LEARNING. Memorizing a list of facts and figures may pave the way for a passing grade, but as much as we may love books and trivia, we take little true pride in such mental drudgery; we're just glad to have passed. Real learning comes when we get our hands dirty: endless hours of building Legos teaching us about structural engineering; summer jobs at the cash register teaching us how to interact as an adult with strangers; college internships at the office showing us how different our chosen field looks in practice than it did on paper. Through the knuckle-rapping pains of experience, we absorb knowledge in a tangible, useful way, not simply learning how things are done but how to do them—and then, how to do them *better*. If we're paying attention, then before long, we start trying to innovate; we break down walls and change our piece of the world while we're at it. We become not just *smart*—that and a quarter will buy you a gumball—but *competent*. And if there's one thing geeks strive for, it's to be more capable than the norm. Thus, we wax.

Mr. Miyagi, the guru in *The Karate Kid* (1984), was portrayed by Pat Morita, who went on to delight geeks by lampooning the role in the cartoon *Robot Chicken*.

"THAT IS MOST OF IT, BEING A WIZARD—SEEING AND LISTENING. THE REST IS TECHNIQUE."

—SCHMENDRICK THE MAGICIAN, *THE LAST UNICORN*

EVEN A STOPPED CLOCK is right twice a day, and in *The Last Unicorn*, Schmendrick the Magician manages to hit on more than one home truth amid his self-doubt and suspicion. His struggles to channel and control his magic form a through-line of the novel, though he sums them up in this single throwaway comment that strikes at the heart of the problem for many of us: knowing when to listen, and then—when the time to talk arrives—how to be really heard. Of seeing and listening, too much praise cannot be said (one need only look at any YouTube comments section to understand the value of restraint). When you're setting out to learn a new skill, attentive observation will do you more good than any other single training tool. The patience to absorb information before acting is the real art; once you've mastered that, Schmendrick's right—what remains is just details.

Peter S. Beagle's *Last Unicorn* is one of the handful of fantasy classics that's simultaneously considered a classic in a second genre: the pony book. It's as often found on a shelf next to *Black Beauty* and *Misty of Chincoteague* as it is alongside *The Hobbit* or *A Wrinkle in Time*.

"EVEN A MAN WHO IS PURE IN HEART AND SAYS HIS PRAYERS BY NIGHT MAY BECOME A WOLF WHEN THE WOLFBANE BLOOMS AND THE AUTUMN MOON IS BRIGHT."

—ANCIENT GYPSY PROVERB, *THE WOLF MAN*

THAT COUPLET at the start of 1941's *The Wolf Man* begins our brief,* tragic sojourn in the brief, tragic life of Larry Talbot, a good man whose pure heart wasn't enough to stop an unfortunate encounter with the business end of a werewolf from saddling him with a very hairy problem. So effectively did writer Curt Siodmak weave the mystery and mysticism of extant werewolf lore into his tale that, even today, many viewers fail to realize that he conjured the proverb entirely from his imagination. What Siodmak's poem signifies is the omnipresent fear we all carry deep inside us that, irrespective of the person we've tried to be or the life we've tried to lead, circumstances outside our control might force us to do or be something terrible—and we might ultimately be powerless to stop it.

---

*Brief, that is, until the first of several sequels came along two years later.

"THAT RUG REALLY TIED THE ROOM TOGETHER."

—THE DUDE, *THE BIG LEBOWSKI*

IF YOUR HOUSE WAS ON FIRE and you could grab only one thing before running to safety, what would it be? Tough decision? Not for the Dude. For him, that rug is a talisman as powerful and mythic as Luke Skywalker's lightsaber or Indiana Jones's fedora, and his stalwart devotion to that artifact provides some insight into why the character resonates. We've been conditioned to think of our movie heroes as quick thinking, forceful, and otherwise action-oriented, but the Dude represents a pointed inversion of the classic heroic paradigm. He's our unfettered id brought to bedraggled, beer-bellied life. There's a primal simplicity to the Dude's personal code of honor that we all can relate to—and many of us wish we could embody. Even when offered a cut of the stolen money he's found, he says, "All the Dude ever wanted was his rug back. Not greedy." He remains utterly, defiantly true to himself even in the face of an increasing unhinged, nonsensical modern world. Now that's some good stuff, Dude.

Jeff Bridges may not be the cultural signifier that Johnny Depp's presence in a film is, but his offbeat selection of roles—The Dude, *Tron*'s Kevin Flynn, *Iron Man*'s Obadiah Stane, *Starman*'s titular alien—definitely marks him as a geek star.

"WORST. EPISODE. EVER."

—COMIC BOOK GUY, *THE SIMPSONS*

"BAZINGA!"

—SHELDON, *THE BIG BANG THEORY*

I F GEEKS ARE ANYTHING, WE ARE OPINIONATED. We wield our views like +1 spiked clubs, casting judgment upon throwaway entertainment as if we were debating scripture *(ahem)*. Those of us who've prowled Internet forums and chat rooms don't just know people like *The Simpsons'* infamous Comic Book Guy, we've *been* them. We walk a fine line between commendable passion for that which we love—starships, superpowers, costumes, fantastic stories—and an almost frightening militancy about the Right Way to Enjoy Them. It's part of what makes us who we are. The Comic Book Guy is revolting not simply because he's loathsome—though he is—but because in our worst moments we, too, can be blindly critical and socially inept. Thankfully for the modern geek, those moments are rarer than they used to be. We long ago crawled out of the basement, took hold of popular culture, and developed the ability to laugh at the image of who we collectively once were.

And yet—sometimes we backslide.

One of geekdom's most visible ambassadors this decade, *The Big Bang Theory*'s Sheldon Cooper is a theoretical physicist who has mastered everything from a prepuberty Ph.D. to the rules of that classic game, Rock, Paper, Scissors, Lizard, Spock. Lifting the old stereotype of the asexual braniac to new heights, Sheldon is a derisive, hygienic, methodical academic who nonetheless benefits greatly from the company of his friends. On paper, he's exactly the person many geeks would point to as a flag-bearer. But as the show's ongoing narrative evolved, the other characters' jabs at Sheldon's expense became something he increasingly played into: His fastidiousness became infantilization, his wry observations started to sound like full-on pompous taunts, and his inside jokes turned into shorthand punch lines to any scene the writers couldn't end coherently. (Lookin' at you, "Bazinga.") Geeks of the world, don't let this happen to you. We know you love to revel in

your geekiness, but it's easy to slip to the dark side; try hard not to turn into a caricature of yourself. And if you *must* have a signature catchphrase, for God's sake, try to keep an eye on how often you're saying it.

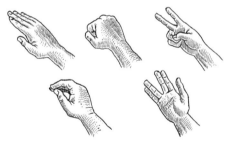

TV producers, take note: Geeks know when you're laughing with us and when you're laughing at us. Sheldon and Comic Book Guy: with us. Steve Urkel: at us.

"FEAR IS THE MIND-KILLER. FEAR IS THE LITTLE-DEATH THAT BRINGS TOTAL OBLITERATION."

—BENE GESSERIT LITANY AGAINST FEAR, *DUNE*

SHE'S THERE, across the room, and her hair is long and it's lovely, and so is she, and you keep stealing glances, you can't even control them, and every time she glances back you avert your gaze because, dear lord, if her eyes were to meet yours. If she could see into yours, she'd know. She'd know what you're feeling and thinking, and that would be so unbearably embarrassing. Your friends nudge. *Go, go,* they say. You can't. Your limbs are frozen, your tongue fat and heavy and swollen. *Go talk to her,* they say. But you won't. You are afraid, and in your fear you've already failed. You know she is already lost to you—or. *Or.* Or maybe you can suppress that fear. Can think, act, do, *talk*; can embrace reason and confidence over raw emotion. Can just go ahead and talk to her, so then maybe, maybe, she'll talk back to you. And you can smile.

Frank Herbert's groundbreaking science-fiction classic *Dune* (1965) was rejected twelve times. Herbert did not let fear of failure prevent him from continuing to send the book out until he found a publisher who believed in it.

"IF MY DOCTOR TOLD ME I HAD ONLY SIX MINUTES TO LIVE, I WOULDN'T BROOD. I'D TYPE A LITTLE FASTER."

—ISAAC ASIMOV

THAT ASIMOV meant what he said is plain to see in the immense library of knowledge and wisdom he imparted to us during his extraordinary lifetime—a library we'll likely continue to benefit from for time immemorial. But you don't have to be Isaac Asimov to understand his broader point. From the moment we're born, the clock begins to tick, daring us to accomplish all that we need to before that last grain of sand drops through the hourglass. Whether, per Asimov's hypothetical, we know how much time we have left, the knowledge that we're engaged in a race we've been engineered to lose can become reason for despair or a clarion call to action. For anyone who's ever been driven by the creative impulse—by the all-encompassing need to take what's inside and put it out there—Asimov's words don't merely ring true; they carry the weight of gospel.

During the 1960s and '70s, Asimov's huge output as popular science writer, best-selling novelist, and futurism lecturer made him a particularly high-profile ambassador for geekdom. In today's splintered media world, that role may never again be so thoroughly captured by a single person.

"SNOZZBERRIES? WHO EVER HEARD OF A SNOZZBERRY?"

—VERUCA SALT, CHARLIE AND THE CHOCOLATE FACTORY

BRATDOM. The four kids adventuring alongside Charlie Bucket in Roald Dahl's master piece were part of it, and when spoiled-rotten-girl Veruca famously uttered this sneering inquiry, it epitomized an idea that recurs regularly in the sacred texts of geek wisdom: Being a know-it-all isn't smart; it's a sign of closed-mindedness. What the brats in life fail to grasp is that the trails of history are blazed not by those who cling to what *is*, but by those who dare to seek out what *might be*. We could offer examples of such folks, the ones who proclaimed their righteousness most belligerently, but history's ultimate judgment can be found in the fact that their names have largely been forgotten—whereas the names of Copernicus, Galileo, and other such curious truth seekers will be enshrined for eternity. As Veruca Salt is hoisted by her self-possessed petard, she reminds us of the simple lesson that believing your own press is dangerous. Despite her loud mouthings to the contrary, there really *were* snozzberries in Wonka's world—just as there really did turn out to be planets and atoms and quarks in ours. We just have to be open to finding them.

There are four Veruca Salts: the one in Roald Dahl's book (1964), the one in the classic movie (1971), the one in the remade movie (2005), and the Chicago indie-rock band who borrowed her name in 1993 and are still making music today.

"TO ERR IS HUMAN; TO REALLY SCREW UP REQUIRES THE ROOT PASSWORD."

—COMPUTER GEEK TRUISM

POOR WIL WHEATON. He came back from a postadolescent slump as a seemingly over-the-hill child actor to have a triumphant second act as one of the most popular bloggers on the Internet. He spent years rebuilding his mojo at wilwheaton.net. And then, one day in September 2005, he decided to climb down into the code and fiddle with his database—and in an instant, his digital world was kaplooey. Borkded. *Over.* Fortunately for Wil, Google can be most forgiving, and although wilwheaton.typepad.com may not glide off the tongue as euphoniously as his original website did, it's easily found. However, unlike our virtual existences online, a human life has no reset button. In real life, things can be broken irreparably and irreplaceably—a treasured heirloom, a marriage, a nation. So before yielding to the impulse to poke at the soft underbelly of things, it's worth asking: Do you know how not to break that? Are you *sure*?

The root is the all-access user account that can control all the files in a Unixlike computer operating system. Wil's database snafu involved a different system, MySQL. Lest you think we're fake geeks, we point out the technical difference while making the fundamentally sound analogy.

"WHY, HELLO, CLARICE."
—HANNIBAL LECTER, *THE SILENCE OF THE LAMBS*

"IF YOU ONLY KNEW THE POWER OF THE DARK SIDE."
—DARTH VADER, *THE EMPIRE STRIKES BACK*

"STEP INTO MY PARLOR, said the spider to the fly." What did Clarice Starling feel as she set down that dank prison hallway to her first encounter with Hannibal Lecter? Probably the same thing we felt as we accompanied her: terror, revulsion, and . . . curiosity. That's always the appeal of evil. It's the temptation of the forbidden, the allure of the illicit, and even though our rational side knows that no good can come from that path, there's another side that longs to push the boundaries to see what happens. The slippery slope is a cliché because it's real: one moral compromise can easily lead to another, and another. And whether we're talking about fictional characters like Lecter and Anakin Skywalker or real-life scenarios like the animal-torturing child who grows up to be an abusive parent, history is replete with the testimonials of those who've taken things one step too far. Yet still we persist in looking the devil in the eyes—perhaps to prove to ourselves that we can. That's why Agent Starling keeps going back even as Lecter pulls his knot of terrifying mind games ever tighter. And let's be honest: It's also why we keep watching. The sequel to *The Silence of the Lambs* wasn't called *Clarice*, after all.

In *The Silence of the Lambs*, the interrogation scenes were filmed in the bowels of Pittsburgh's Soldiers and Sailors Memorial building, just up the road from the geek mecca of Carnegie Mellon University.

"NO, I NEVER DID IT!"

—CLAIRE, *THE BREAKFAST CLUB*

C LAIRE THOUGHT SHE WAS HOT STUFF, didn't she? That is, until she was finally worn down and had to admit to being the inexperienced, insecure girl she'd tried to conceal. Whether we cheered at seeing Ms. Perfect taken down a peg or sympathized with the persona she felt forced to put on doesn't matter. What does matter is that Claire, along with the other misfits of *The Breakfast Club*, showed us that we weren't alone in seeing through the phony B.S. that was high school. Sure, we all had our cliques and circles and groups—and heaven forbid they should ever intersect with another—but hell, if the hot, rich, redheaded darling was in truth an insecure, awkward teen, too, where does that leave us losers who felt lucky to get to second base by sixteen? It leaves us realizing that those people in school we thought were so, so, so much cooler and hipper and more with it than we were . . . weren't. Because Claire? She never did it.

The Breakfast Club (1982) costarred Judd Nelson, whose geek credentials were further enhanced when he starred as Hot Rod in *Transformers: The Movie* (1986).

"NO MATTER WHERE YOU GO . . . THERE YOU ARE."

—BUCKAROO BANZAI,
THE ADVENTURES OF BUCKAROO BANZAI ACROSS THE 8TH DIMENSION

A S NOTED IN THE INTRODUCTION, statements uttered as jokes can be taken far more seriously than ever intended. Heroic polymath Buckaroo Banzai, while taking a break from his duties as a nuclear-physicist-brain-surgeon-action-hero to play some piano-bar ballads in his alternate guise as a rock star, offered up this little gem to settle down an unruly crowd. Screenwriter Earl Mac Rauch employed it for humor, befuddling the audience both onscreen and off with what sounded like a semantically empty phrase, a sorta-Zen-shaped existential tautology that seems hilarious in its unhelpfulness. But it does mean something real—which is easier to grasp if, in the second clause, you remove the emphasis from the word *there* and put it on the word *you*, instead. The saying isn't intended to mean "Everyplace is a place" but, rather, "*You* can't run away from yourself." You are the single common factor in every situation—so perhaps the best way to improve your surroundings is to improve yourself.

Buckaroo Banzai (1984) may be the ultimate achievement in deadpan storytelling: Even dedicated science-fiction fans often call it an awful mess on their first viewing, only to watch it again and realize that the filmmakers were engaged in subtle comedy all along.

"THERE ARE VOCAL QUALITIES PECULIAR TO MEN, AND VOCAL QUALITIES PECULIAR TO BEASTS; AND IT IS TERRIBLE TO HEAR THE ONE WHEN THE SOURCE SHOULD YIELD THE OTHER."

—H. P. LOVECRAFT, *THE CALL OF CTHULHU*

IS THERE ANYTHING that can strike fear into our hearts more effectively than seeing, experiencing, or even just hearing someone's humanity stripped from them? The very idea of uncontrollable fear chills us, because it underscores just how tenuous our grasp on our humanity truly is. We tell ourselves we are not beasts—we are human beings. Fear, though, is a primal thing. Civilized as we may be, fear has a way of worming under our skin and burrowing into the soft, fleshy parts of us we pretend aren't there. Your childhood poison may have been the dark, or heights, or spiders, or clowns, but the results were always the same. Loss of control. The feeling that even when you *knew* you had nothing to fear, your body and mind could paralyze you. In those moments you were not human, you were beast. And more than any darkness or clown or spider, that's what frightened you the most: the terror of losing yourself to something hidden within.

H. P. Lovecraft had lots of friends and interacted with them mostly through written correspondence; he also wrote horror stories featuring thinly disguised versions of his own childhood imaginary characters. In short: He was the original emo geek.

"THE DANGER MUST BE GROWING FOR THE ROWERS KEEP ON ROWING AND THEY'RE CERTAINLY NOT SHOWING ANY SIGNS THAT THEY ARE SLOWING!"

—WILLY WONKA, *WILLY WONKA AND THE CHOCOLATE FACTORY*

T HE EXTERNAL FORCES that shake up our lives and plunge us headlong into trouble are often far less worrisome than the trouble we cause for ourselves. That's because we're often our own worst enemy, accelerating trouble or worsening a coming train wreck by making poor (and often selfish) decisions. It almost seems to defy common sense. With foreknowledge of growing danger, you'd think our instinct would be to be more cautious, more careful, more mindful of the things we do. Instead, humans do the opposite. We're rash. We're reckless. We're selfish. Even knowing that bad times are ahead offers little protection against this self-sabotage. Willy Wonka knew it, teasing the children in his chocolate factory about the mounting danger in front of them, taunting them with looming troubles ahead—and ultimately confirming his suspicion that most of these kids would be sunk not by the depths of his wondrous chocolate river, but by the foolishness of their own actions. The rowers can keep on rowing and the danger may be growing, but the biggest dangers we face are often our own poor choices.

Geek-war alert: We hereby declare that this scene in 1971's *Willy Wonka and the Chocolate Factory* proves that—our fondness for Johnny Depp aside—Gene Wilder will never be supplanted as the one true Wonka.

"BUT I WAS GOING INTO TOSCHE STATION TO PICK UP SOME POWER CONVERTERS!"

—LUKE SKYWALKER, *STAR WARS*

"WHY ME?"

—GARION, *PAWN OF PROPHECY*

OH, WHINY SUBURBAN TEENAGERS. Can you not just shut up and do what needs doing? If you could, you would be heroic romantic figures; just look at Westley from *The Princess Bride* (p. 72), who, like you, was just a poor boy from a rinky-dink farm right outside of town. But instead you spend half your time moping, and, we have to tell you, it's not particularly attractive. Hey, Luke, you know why you didn't get the girl? It's not because she's your sister. No, George decided to *make* her your sister because it was painfully obvious that the ladies were hot for Han Solo, who, for all his problems with dodging the collection agencies, at least didn't bitch about it. Likewise your medieval-fantasy counterpart Garion from David Eddings's *Belgariad*, whose sword was just as big and glowy, whose princess was just as opinionated, and who let grownups tell him what to do even while he complained every step of the way. Here's the deal, teenagers: If you have real problems in your life, then of course yes, call for help. But if you're just *bored*? If you just don't feel like doing your chores? Quit your yapping.

Unlike lots of 1980s epic fantasy that ripped off Tolkien, Eddings's *Belgariad* read more like a fuller, richer *Star Wars* saga dressed up in Arthurian drag.

"YOU KEEP USING THAT WORD. I DO NOT THINK IT MEANS WHAT YOU THINK IT MEANS."

—INIGO MONTOYA, *THE PRINCESS BRIDE*

HERE'S WHY WE LOVE INIGO MONTOYA: there is not a cynical bone in his body. When the mercenary boss Fezzini kept screaming that it was "inconceivable!" his schemes could be defeated, the little loudmouth knew precisely what the word meant—he was simply such an irrepressibly arrogant ass that he was determined to insist the word was warranted when it really, really wasn't. Inigo could have pointed that out. But he didn't. He gave Fezzini the benefit of the doubt and suggested that perhaps, just possibly, the pompous Sicilian was confused about his dictionary definitions. Whether Inigo was being sincere or incredibly subtly sarcastic, he sounded sincere—thus graciously giving Fezzini a chance to step back from his idiocy and rethink things. That Fezzini didn't take that chance meant his fate was inevitable; that Inigo offered it meant he was willing to consider all things possible. Until proven otherwise, of course.

William Goldman, writer of *Butch Cassidy and the Sundance Kid*, wrote both the novel and the movie version of *The Princess Bride*; it may be the most perfectly cross-medium-rendered story in history and, not coincidentally, one of the most frequently quoted.

"CAN IT BE DONE, FATHER?
CAN A MAN CHANGE THE STARS?"
—WILLIAM THATCHER, *A KNIGHT'S TALE*

THIS QUESTION, THE CENTRAL THESIS of the romantic jousting comedy *A Knight's Tale*, gives us an excellent example of (a) how easy it is to conflate the modern science of astronomy with the archaic practice of astrology and (b) how poetically satisfying it can be to do so as long as you're not taking it too seriously. When the motif is first introduced, a grizzled old squire tells the young peasant boy William that he can no sooner become a nobleman than he can change the stars—a clear reference to the astronomical fact that the stars, a fact of nature, will be as they are and do as they do, with no relation to the actions of humans muddling along on earth. The boy's father then tells him that if a man is brave and determined enough, he can accomplish anything he sets his mind to. William takes this advice to heart and dedicates his life to "changing his stars"; with that possessive pronoun added, the stars cease to be a metaphor for the implacable universe and become a reflection of the would-be knight's personal destiny. William, in all his lack of education, takes for granted the astrological model of the heavens as our controlling power—and then, at the same stroke, turns it upside down, insisting that he'll master his own fate and the heavens be damned. It's an elegant lesson in the power of myth and metaphor in shaping a narrative—whether that story is the one you're watching or the one you're living.

"WHAT'S THE POINT IN BEING GROWN UP IF YOU CAN'T BE CHILDISH SOMETIMES?"

—THE DOCTOR, *DOCTOR WHO*

"SECOND STAR TO THE RIGHT, AND STRAIGHT ON TILL MORNING."

—PETER PAN, *PETER PAN*

A T SOME UNDEFINED POINT in time between 2006 and 2010, *Doctor Who* became the new *Star Trek*. Which is to say, it ceased to be that goofy British sci-fi show with the laughable special effects that even most American nerds had never really watched, and instead it became the new geek pop-culture touchstone, general knowledge of which marks someone irrefutably as one of the tribe. Why did this happen? In part, it was because there was a void—J. J. Abrams notwithstanding, *Trek* ran out of steam years back—and, in part it was because the Internet-fueled ease of viewing a BBC show in real time, instead of months or years later on PBS, finally made the show widely accessible in the States. But there's something deeper at work, too: the Doctor is a hero for our times. Where latter-day *Trek* gave us an engineer's vision of the future, *Doctor Who* and its semianarchic, semiabsurdist mad-genius time traveler in a galaxy-hopping police telephone box reflect a present era so casually insane that it often feels like the best we can do to overcome our sticky dilemmas is to take a deep breath, think hard, giggle nervously, and try something crazy from the weird part of our brains while crossing our fingers and swearing love and good wishes to the world at large. The Doctor represents not only "the triumph of intellect and romance over brute force and cynicism," as Craig Ferguson so eloquently put it, but, more specifically, our unsullied, childlike vision of a universe where all things ought to be possible. He's a grown-up Peter Pan, always collecting new young friends and teaching them to fight the good fight on Earth rather than in Neverland. That's a pretty great feat for a 900-year-old alien.

"I'M CRUSHING YOUR HEAD!"

—MR. TYZIK, *THE KIDS IN THE HALL*

IT'S ALL ABOUT PERSPECTIVE. Can you crush some-one's head between your thumb and forefinger? Of course not . . . unless you stand ten feet away and hold your hand up to your own eye, in which case, yes, their head is *clearly* a mere grape to be squashed between your massive, unstoppable digits. It's an illusion, naturally, but illusion is a powerful tool. Geek tales often consciously use this kind of Escheresque frame-of-reference shift—for instance, when *Doctor Who*'s TARDIS can fit an end-lessly huge spaceship interior inside the door of a four-foot-by-four-foot-by-seven-foot box, because, you see, the inside dimen-sion is in a realm far distant from the outside dimension. Or when Obi-Wan Kenobi told Luke that his earlier assertion that "Darth Vader betrayed and murdered your father" wasn't a *lie* so much as a spiritual interpretation of the truth. Getting a different perspective on things is one of the best ways there is to kick your imagination or your problem-solving brain into high gear; that's why compa-nies hire outside consultants or take the staff out of the office on retreats to ponder the challenges that lie before them. And it's just as helpful in your daily life—so, today, why not walk a different route? Maybe you'll see something you've been missing. And that something probably won't crush your head—but, you know, it might just blow your mind.

"THIS MUST BE THURSDAY. I NEVER COULD GET THE HANG OF THURSDAYS."

—ARTHUR DENT, *THE HITCHHIKER'S GUIDE TO THE GALAXY*

I N ARTHUR'S CASE, Thursday began with the demolition of his house, continued with the demolition of the entire planet Earth, and eventually culminated in him getting tossed into deep space without a spacesuit. Most people's Thursdays can't compare . . . and yet it's not hard to relate to what Arthur was going through. Because every day of the week presents its own unique problems. Monday, obviously, is the beginning of the work week—*ugh*. Tuesday is almost worse, because it's practically as far away from Friday night as Monday is, but without the satisfaction of being able to complain about it being Monday. Wednesday is the day when you realize that the glorious things you intended to accomplish this week probably aren't all going to happen. Thursday we've discussed already. Friday might be the very worst, because you have a sense that people are having huge amounts of fun on Friday evening, and if you're not, something must be wrong with you. Saturday is wonderful, unless you have chores that need to be done—and you do. And Sunday? Sunday is the Wednesday of the weekend, except that on Wednesday at least half the week is over, and on Sunday it's all ahead of you. Let's face it: Arthur was doomed no matter what day the Vogons blew up the Earth.

II.
FORM FEET AND LEGS

(WISDOM ABOUT RELATIONSHIPS)

"YOU—YOU'VE GOT ME? WHO'S GOT YOU?"

—LOIS LANE, *SUPERMAN: THE MOTION PICTURE*

PEOPLE GREATER THAN ourselves do what they do with no wires and no safety net. They fly free, able to accomplish things that we not only can't do, but that we can't even *imagine* doing. But this doesn't just apply to those who perform astonishing feats of derring-do. Think of a parent—maybe your own, maybe a single mother, maybe a struggling couple. On a daily basis, they swoop up beneath their children, holding them aloft, saving them from hitting the ground too hard when they fall off one of those metaphorical skyscrapers whose edge they hadn't seen coming. Quietly, parents are  all Supermen and Superwomen holding up their Lois Lanes and Jimmy Olsens—and the same truth applies to anyone whose efforts support another. Enter Lois's question: If all these people have got her covered, who's covering them? When it comes to the unsung heroes of the world, the answer all too often is, "Nobody." In the real world, they don't have a Superman of their own. That they persevere nonetheless makes them superheroes by any measure.

Superman: The Motion Picture (1978) marked the introduction into the Superman mystique of such concepts as the cold and sterile planet Krypton (in the comics it had been a colorful civilization) and businessman Lex Luthor (in the comics he was a scientist).

"FACE IT, TIGER, YOU JUST HIT THE JACKPOT!"

—MARY JANE WATSON, *THE AMAZING SPIDER-MAN*

ONE OF THE MOST dramatic entrances in comic-book history was more than the introduction of a vivacious, sexy redhead—though it certainly was that!—it was also a lesson in the nature of expectations. For months Peter Parker's elderly aunt had been nattering on about her friend's niece, Mary Jane Watson, but Peter just rolled his eyes and brushed off the old bird's ham-fisted attempt at matchmaking with nary a second thought. He never expected that Mary Jane would be so WOW. That's the thing about life: We find gems in the most unexpected places. Always down on his luck, confused and confounded by the opposite sex, and burdened with personal problems that never seemed to go away, a guy like Peter Parker doesn't expect much good to come his way. Do any of us? Experience teaches us young the danger of being eternal optimists. Yet there she was. The famous comic-book panel of Mary Jane standing in the doorway, a cat-who-ate-the-canary grin on her face while Peter reels, stunned at seeing such a knockout, has come to define having your pessimistic expectations shattered. The jolt of something so happily vibrant is a jackpot, indeed.

One of the bitterest comic-book flamewars of the decade was prompted when Marvel Comics decided to retroactively undo Peter and Mary Jane's two-decade-long marriage via a literal deal with the devil to save Aunt May's life.

"I ASK FOR SO LITTLE. JUST FEAR ME, LOVE ME, DO AS I SAY AND I WILL BE YOUR SLAVE."

—JARETH THE GOBLIN KING, *LABYRINTH*

"YOU HAVE NO POWER OVER ME."

—SARAH, *LABYRINTH*

GIRLHOOD IN GEEKDOM HAS NEVER BEEN EASY. Apart from the usual difficulties of growing up geeky—fitting in, finding oneself, learning that it's okay to be smart and that "eccentric" is in the eye of the beholder—geek girls who are so inclined also have to deal with geek guys. Who are, shall we say, works in progress at that age. Which may be why David Bowie's androgynous, seductive, and artful Goblin King won the hearts and fantasies of so many geek girls. He was a bad boy . . . and yet, a pretty good babysitter. He had a castle inspired by Escher and suggestively talented fingers. And, yeah, he was old enough to be Sarah's grandfather and kind of creepy to boot—but as teen girl fantasy objects go, it could've been worse. Perhaps most important of all, Sarah found that he *had no power over her, other than what she gave him.* It's fascinating to consider just how few fantasy heroines have been able to assert themselves and remain single in the face of a romance. Bucking the trend of the typical Hollywood epic, *Labyrinth* showed a young woman learning to take responsibility for her actions, persevere in an unfair world, and own her sexual identity. She wasn't just a babe—she was the babe with the power.

David Bowie has been an alien (*The Man Who Fell to Earth*, 1976), a Goblin King (*Labyrinth*, 1986), and a human superscientist (*The Prestige*, 2006). His fans were lobbying hard for him to play Elrond in *The Lord of the Rings*, too.

"ELEMENTARY, MY DEAR WATSON!"

—SHERLOCK HOLMES, REPEATEDLY

NO OTHER QUOTE so quickly puts poor Watson in the hot seat, does it? And it's really not fair. The general public perception of Watson as a bumbling oaf couldn't be further from the character who narrates Arthur Conan Doyle's stories, who's both a clever doctor in his own right and more socially perceptive than the genius with whom he keeps company. But sidekick syndrome can be a big damper on any circle of friends. All it takes is one socially unaware friend who's better-versed in something to put the group rudely in their place. That friend has likely explained to you the detailed virtues of, say, shiraz, or Jonathan Demme's film career, or how your iPod *really* works—snidely and at great length, thus killing forever any interest you might have had in it. It can be a lot to take, but Watsons of the world can take heart: Popular culture is beginning to realize that, for all his genius, Sherlock Holmes still didn't know that the earth revolved around the sun, and that Watson saved his pal's bacon more than once. And if you recognize yourself more in Sherlock than in Watson, it might be time for a round of apologies to your social circle.

Testifying once again to the power of mass media, the well-known phrase quoted above is a formulation of the 1929 movie *The Return of Sherlock Holmes*, not of Arthur Conan Doyle's original stories.

"YES. YES, I DID IT. I KILLED YVETTE. I HATED HER, SO . . . *MUCH* . . . IT—IT—THE F—IT—FLAME—FLAMES. FLAMES, ON THE SIDE OF MY FACE."

—MRS. WHITE, *CLUE*

THIS IS HOW LIFE WORKS: We all want to be the butler, but really we're all Mrs. White. Betrayed by the people we trust, sabotaged by those we don't expect, patronized by houseguests, and always on the verge of boiling over— and, finally, feeling as though our feelings are palpable. Of course, few of us ever give in to our darker sides quite as murderously as Mrs. White did; that doesn't mean it's not tempting to tell people exactly what you think of them. That urge for brutal honesty can threaten to overcome all the hard-won social graces we acquire over the years. The good news is, once in a while, that scorched-earth approach can be just what we need to separate ourselves from a bad situation. We recommend, however, that you keep your revenge limited to a few scathing e-mails. These days, not a lot of people buy the "Why don't you come with me to this remote British manor where we can be alone?" approach.

There is hardly a line of dialogue in the entire movie *Clue* (1985) that has not become a cult-classic quote. Kudos to filmmaker Jonathan Lynn.

"HEYYY YOU GUUUUYYS!"

—SLOTH, *THE GOONIES*, CHANNELING *THE ELECTRIC COMPANY*

THE GOONIES isn't the greatest search-for-treasure adventure movie ever made (that's *Raiders of the Lost Ark*), nor is it the greatest group-of-friends-has-their-final-adventure-together movie (that's *Stand by Me*), but it might be the greatest we're-misfits-and-we-belong-together movie. It all comes down to Sloth. He's big, ugly, and maybe a little slow. But he's also loving, and in need of love, and someone who has seen far too much abuse at the hands of others. So when Sloth bellows his proud greeting and jumps into the fray with his newfound friends, it's not just an awesome movie moment, it's a celebration of acceptance for someone who has never before been accepted. Because when you're an outcast crew like the Goonies, you just can't pull the same dirty tricks of shunning and snubbing that other cliques have pulled on you—it would be like stabbing yourself in the heart.

The Electric Company (1971), which Sloth was quoting, may have been one of the most eclectic geek TV shows ever, featuring a PBS version of Spider-Man and launching the career of Morgan Freeman.

"THIS JOB WOULD BE GREAT IF IT WASN'T FOR THE F—ING CUSTOMERS."

—RANDAL GRAVES, *CLERKS*

A S NERDS AND GEEKS, we are often teased in childhood for being so damned smart. As a defense mechanism to help us cope with the accusation that we're not like other people, we come to embrace the idea that most everyone else is dumber than we are. And we grow up sneering at our peers who seem to have an easy time fitting into society, which we declare is because they're *mundane*—even as we secretly resent *them* for how comfortably they all seem to get along with one another. Here's the thing: None of it is true. Those non-nerds? Most of them feel like outsiders, too; they're all just faking it as best they can and trying not to let their insecurities show. So chill out, Randal. The customers in your store only seem so damn stupid because you've spent so long nurturing your own identity as a smartypants. Take a moment to remember the last four stupid things you did, and then be nice to the lady who doesn't understand what it says on the box.

Kevin Smith, writer/director of *Clerks*, may have been the first writer to formally canonize science fiction as the scripture of pop culture, referring to Star Wars as the "Holy Trilogy" in *Chasing Amy* (1997).

"WONDER TWIN POWERS, ACTIVATE!"

—ZAN AND JAYNA, *THE SUPERFRIENDS*

THE PRINCIPAL MESSAGE of the superpowered siblings in this classic cartoon was obvious: We're better when we work together. However, the underlying subtext of the Wonder Twins was more telling: Sometimes, one of you is going to have the ability to turn into every awesome animal ever, and one of you is mostly going to turn into a pail of water and spill all over the place. It's a hard lesson. We all want to think that things even out in the end, and that if someone is more talented in one arena, we'll outdo them in another. Often, that's the

case. But sometimes it's not, and it's then that you have to do the work to realize that friendship—or mystical twin-ship, whatever—builds on the work you do together, rather than on one of you standing out. Besides, sometimes it's a bucket full of water that saves the day. And really the best part of being a Wonder Twin isn't even having the powers. It's sharing a secret with your closest friend.

The Superfriends was TV's original adaptation of DC Comics' *Justice League of America*. But unlike past radio/TV creations, like Jimmy Olsen and Kryptonite, that made their way to the comics page, the Wonder Twins have never become a major part of DC's print mythos.

"FEAR LEADS TO ANGER; ANGER LEADS TO HATE; HATE LEADS TO SUFFERING."

—YODA, *THE PHANTOM MENACE*

YODA was paraphrasing the first great African American geek, George Washington Carver, who said a century ago: "Fear of something is at the root of hate for others, and hate within will eventually destroy the hater." Carver, a scientist plying his trade in a time when the intellectual inferiority of black people was simply assumed, knew something about suffering. Born into slavery, kidnapped as an infant, threatened repeatedly with lynching throughout his life, and rejected from school after school due to his race, Carver eventually went on to become one of the best-known American researchers in the biological and agricultural sciences. Widely rumored to be gay, Carver spent his life confronting and overcoming the fears of others, earning an iconic place in geek history. Yoda might be the fictional guru we like to quote, but Carver is the real one whose life reverberates through our culture.

Look, we all know that *The Phantom Menace* (1999) is not a great movie. But the trailer *was* a great trailer, and this quote was in the trailer. Can't we just pretend that the trailer had a different movie attached to it?

"FORM FEET AND LEGS! FORM ARMS AND BODY! AND I'LL FORM THE HEAD!"

—KEITH, *VOLTRON*

THE WORD *organization*, at its root, means "to make people function like organs." When you're a member of an organization, you and your fellows all fit into a larger system like parts of a body, your individual efforts combining to serve a single specific purpose. *Voltron*, and similar Japanese sci-fi shows such as *Super Sentai* (aka *Power Rangers*), took this concept literally, depicting the adventures of five space-warrior squadron-mates. Each one drove a color-coded combat vehicle that could reconfigure itself into a robotic arm, leg, torso, or head, and all five could then combine into one giant, ass-kicking gestalt of a robot. It's a premise that makes sense coming from a nation famous for its cultural focus on collaboration rather than individualism. The United States, on the other hand, tends to mythologize solo accomplishment, in the arts as well as in business and politics. Heck, even our sports teams win fame mostly for their standout superstars. A lot of American kids don't even play sports—and for them Voltron was a powerfully concretized metaphor for the incredible power of teamwork.

Obscure geek trivia: acclaimed artificial-organ engineer James Antaki, Ph.D., is also the inventor of an electric harmonica—an entirely different kind of "artificial organ."

"SOMETIMES, I DOUBT YOUR COMMITMENT TO SPARKLE MOTION!"

—KITTY, *DONNIE DARKO*

I T SAYS SOMETHING about the power of geek that in a movie about a pessimistic teenage boy who time-travels through parallel universes beside a monstrous seven-foot rabbit, the film's most immortal line is about his little sister's dance troupe. The same geeks' dedication brought this film from the verge of direct-to-DVD obscurity to cult classic; they should be duly proud. Of course, part of this quote's perfection is its perfect storm of relevance to the postmodern era: dead-on suburban satire, overdramatic in-character sincerity, and the comic payoff by the troupe itself. However, the other aspect of Sparkle Motion's enduring popularity is its meme-friendly resilience out of context. Kitty's cry of anguish has been neatly appropriated by geeks to become facetious Internet shorthand for the accusation that someone isn't invested enough in an admittedly frivolous pursuit; it's a beautiful example of how postmodern geekdom can be self-aware enough not to take everything seriously.

Bonus: Sparkle Motion is also the gift that keeps on giving for anyone who wants to take shots at the *Twilight* franchise's glitter-heavy bloodsuckers.

"PINKY, ARE YOU PONDERING WHAT I'M PONDERING?"

—THE BRAIN, *PINKY AND THE BRAIN*

MOST GEEKS have non-geek friends. Inevitably, they sometimes don't know what the heck we're talking about, so most of us have learned how to break down our thought processes for their sakes—to flawlessly translate even the geekiest of concepts into introductory language. This is a variation on the "double consciousness" concept first described by W. E. B. Du Bois (who wrote science fiction as well as activist commentary) in reference to African Americans' need to move between two worlds. In many ways, it's a requirement of any minority population that wants to be accepted by the majority—or at least to be left in peace. But sometimes we get tired of simul-translating our own conversations. Sometimes we just want to relax and be ourselves, even around our non-geeky friends, and sometimes, justified or not, we feel as though *we're* the ones who always have to do the interpreting. That's why so many of us loved it when the Brain didn't bother, blurting out theories and plans so byzantine no one could possibly follow them—and we loved even more that Pinky didn't demand an explanation. It's nice to have a friend who'll meet you halfway.

The Brain was voiced by Canadian actor Maurice LaMarche, who's also *Futurama*'s Kif Kroker and *The Real Ghostbusters*' Egon Spengler. Fans are divided on the question of whether he or Vincent D'Onofrio does a better Orson Welles impression.

"MY NAME IS SAYID JARRAH, AND I AM A TORTURER."

—SAYID JARRAH, *LOST*, "ONE OF THE THEM"

I N A SHOW that survived and thrived for six labyrinthine seasons by asking viewers to question long-cemented notions of "us" and "them," no character was a better exemplar of this than Sayid Jarrah. The Iraqi. The Muslim. The self-proclaimed "torturer." Although a Manichean media culture of prefigured heroes and villains could easily have conditioned us to hate and fear such a figure, over the course of the show's run we also came to know Sayid the technician, Sayid the soldier, Sayid the lover, and even Sayid the poet. All added facets to the character, and all illuminated for us the fluid nature of identity. In the end, "us" and "them" are arbitrary labels, but it was through the specificities, the complexities of Sayid's character that he achieved a kind of universality, painting a portrait of an individual driven by his own demons trying to do right by himself and others—in other words, someone just like "us."

The editors would like to take this space to ask anyone who has not yet watched *Lost* to do so . . . but only the first couple seasons. Don't be a sadist like we were and watch to the bitter end. You'll regret it. Really.

"I'M SORRY, DAVE, I'M AFRAID I CAN'T DO THAT."

—HAL 9000, *2001: A SPACE ODYSSEY*

THE most famous computer malfunction in cinematic history saw HAL, the artificial intelligence running the fictional American spacecraft *Discovery*, go crazy and murder most of the astronauts on board before they reached Jupiter. The sequel revealed that HAL's psychotic break was caused by an irreconcilable conflict between contradictory instruc-tions: "his" basic purpose of accurately analyzing information for the crew, and his top-secret government directive to conceal *Discovery*'s true mission from them. You have to feel sorry for HAL—he was experiencing the same ominous dread that infects any of us when someone puts us in the uncomfortable situation of having to lie on their behalf. The classmate who wants to use you as an alibi to cover her misbehaving ways; the spouse who invents a fictional emergency to get out of visiting the in-laws; the friend who doesn't want you to tell his wife he's leaving her, never mind that she's your friend, too. What do you do when your loyalty is at odds with your sense of what's right? HAL's story doesn't offer an answer, but it does illuminate what a good idea it is to avoid such situations in the first place.

In the book version of *2001*, *Discovery*'s mission is to reach Saturn by way of Jupiter; in the film, the ship is simply headed to Jupiter. Author Arthur C. Clarke yielded to the film's popularity for the sequel novel *2010* and just went with Jupiter.

"I STAYED UP ALL NIGHT PLAYING POKER WITH TAROT CARDS. I GOT A FULL HOUSE AND FOUR PEOPLE DIED."

—STEVEN WRIGHT

STANDUP COMEDIANS don't just stand on a stage a few nights a week; they stand apart from humanity every day. Though we think of professional funnymen as a breed all their own, at heart they're pretty much like all the other people who become writers, whether novelists or news reporters. They are outside observers, watching and taking notes on all this fuss the rest of us engage in, all while preparing to turn around and show us something so deeply true about ourselves that we' just have to react. Steven Wright is the ultimate exemplar of this kind of emotional detachment; his voice during performance as he mumbles his way through one pithy ten-second joke-concept at a time is distant, muted—almost robotic. But when he delivers this one, you can hear surprise register as he hits the punch line, as if with a simple rising inflection he wants to convey: *Hey, this isn't all a theoretical exercise, after all; I really am connected to the rest of the world!* In an era when Internet socializing allows us to reduce our mental picture of our fellow human beings to nothing more than a name and a postage-stamp-size picture on a screen, it's a lesson well worth remembering.

Tarot cards formed the mythic centerpiece of comic auteur Alan Moore's 1999 science-fantasy series *Promethea*, about a superheroine conjured from the realm of pure narrative imagination.

"SUGAR. SPICE.
AND EVERYTHING NICE.
THESE WERE THE
INGREDIENTS CHOSEN
TO CREATE THE PERFECT
LITTLE GIRLS.
BUT PROFESSOR UTONIUM
ACCIDENTALLY ADDED
AN EXTRA INGREDIENT
TO THE CONCOCTION . . .
CHEMICAL X."

—OPENING NARRATION, *THE POWERPUFF GIRLS*

GEEK WOMEN—*real* geek women, that is, not the booth babes or big-eyed anime schoolgirls who dominate the imaginations of heterosexual geek men—are built of strange stuff. Consider what it takes to resist the pervasive sexism of American society, which pressures all women to value themselves on appearance alone. Geek women, however, demand to be recognized for their brains. They want to be admired for their l33t skills in gaming, their clever code constructions, their solid engineering designs. In other words, they're not all that different from geek guys . . . which makes things awkward when they turn on a video game or open a comic book to find female characters with size 44F breasts and waists so tiny there can't possibly be functioning organs in there. That's why the Powerpuff Girls are such a viciously ironic thrill. The Girls don't look human; they don't have the same proportions as the other characters in the cartoon, or even fingers and toes. It's basically a juvenile twist on the way adult women are generally depicted for men's viewing pleasure—and yet, the Girls *kicked ass*. They whomped jerks and monsters. They looked out for one another. And for the few men in their lives who saw them as individuals and valued them for their personhood, they made the world a better place.

The Powerpuff Girls ran for six years (1998–2004)—longer than the age of the titular characters.

"UNTIL A MAN IS TWENTY-FIVE, HE STILL THINKS, EVERY SO OFTEN, THAT UNDER THE RIGHT CIRCUMSTANCES HE COULD BE THE BADDEST MOTHERF—ER IN THE WORLD."

—NEAL STEPHENSON, *SNOW CRASH*

THE MALE GEEK has largely made it a point of pride to distance himself from the stereotypical tough guys of the world. But the male geek is deluding himself. Fact is, we're not all that far removed from each other, geeks and jocks. Stephenson nails why: The notion that, if circumstances were right, we could be "The Man" is the impulse that fuels male fantasies, from Mickey Mantle to Batman, from Muhammad Ali to Casanova. Nerd or not, men dream of inspiring awe in those around them—and by "awe" we mean "adoration," and by "those around them" we mean "mostly women." What separates male peer groups is the form these dreams of prowess take. The athlete dreams of attainable feats of athleticism; the geek, lacking such physical agency, just goes ahead and fantasizes much bigger. Win the playoffs? *Pffffft*. We're here to save the universe! Even if that's just our own self-doubt pushing us to overcompensate in the realm of imagination, one thing is clear: There are times when, no matter how outlandish it seems, we're determined to believe that maybe, just maybe, we' truly are capable of becoming the badass we dream of.

Stephenson's *Baroque Cycle* has become known as his magnum opus, but *Snow Crash* (1992) made his name as one of the icons of cyberpunk.

"I HAVE BEEN, AND ALWAYS SHALL BE, YOUR FRIEND."

—SPOCK, *STAR TREK II: THE WRATH OF KHAN*

SPOCK'S DYING WORDS, uttered upon sacrificing his own life to save the lives of his friends Kirk and McCoy and all their crewmates, are a favorite quote used to express geek camaraderie. But here's a question that's rarely asked: What made these guys such great friends, anyway? It wasn't just the fact of their shared experiences on the *Enterprise*; after all, you probably have coworkers you wouldn't give your life for. No, what brought Star Trek's trinity together was that, though all three were men of great passion and great intellectual achievement, they channeled those impulses differently. Scientist Spock carried the flag for the rational approach to life; "just a country doctor" McCoy championed the empathic approach; and Kirk their captain mediated the two, navigating the right blend of emotion and critical thinking to make their way through any situation. We should all have friends who are similar enough to relate, but different enough to challenge us—who respect our thoughts and opinions even while they're telling us how wrong we are.

Daily Show correspondent and "PC Guy" John Hodgman quoted this line to President Obama while grilling him on his geek knowledge at the 2009 Radio and Television Correspondents Dinner.

"DO NOT MEDDLE IN THE AFFAIRS OF WIZARDS, FOR THEY ARE SUBTLE AND QUICK TO ANGER."

—GILDOR, *THE LORD OF THE RINGS*

O N THE SURFACE, this warning to the hobbits of *The Lord of the Rings* appears to be another manifestation of Tolkien's views on social and class structure (most notably on display in Sam's subservience to Frodo). Gildor implies that the wise and great cannot be understood by the merely ordinary, who would do best not to interfere with their betters. Yet look closer: By the end of the story, Gildor and the elves have departed Middle Earth, and the very affairs the hobbits were warned not to meddle in would have gone badly were it not *for* their meddling. The warning, then, is not to avoid crossing paths with your betters—in fact, it's not about one's "betters" at all. Gildor may have meant it that way, but Tolkien clearly didn't. Rather, the point is that to get involved with those who carry the weight of responsibility on their shoulders is to take on a measure of that responsibility ourselves. Meddle in the affairs of wizards at your own peril, lest you find yourself carrying a similar burden.

This saying has spawned a favorite geek parody: "Do not meddle in the affairs of dragons, for you are crunchy and taste good with ketchup."

"NO, MR. BOND. I EXPECT YOU TO DIE!"

—AURIC GOLDFINGER, *GOLDFINGER*

THERE'S JUST NO TALKING TO SOME PEOPLE. Oh, you can try. You can form your arguments, bring your evidence, and go in with as open a mind as possible. But at some point you have to realize the other person isn't interested in a meeting of the minds. For James Bond, that realization probably hit when he was strapped to a solid gold table by the dastardly Goldfinger with a laser beam inexorably advancing toward his unmentionables. We may never be in a similarly precarious position against a similarly implacable foe, but at some point in our lives we'll likely square off against a rival who doesn't believe in fair play, can't be appealed to or reasoned with, and doesn't just want to win but wants you to lose. While Agent 007 finessed some very quick thinking to stay the hand of his erstwhile executioner, sometimes the quickest thinking of all is to simply recognize the Goldfingers in our lives before we end up staring at that laser.

The laser in *Goldfinger* (1964) was a clever atomic-age updating of the tension-filled threat found in Edgar Allan Poe's *Pit and the Pendulum* (1842).

"AS YOU WISH."

—WESTLEY, *THE PRINCESS BRIDE*

"IT WAS BEAUTY KILLED THE BEAST."

—CARL DENHAM, *KING KONG*

WHY DO WOMEN love *The Princess Bride* so much? Here's a thought: because its hero, Westley, is able to simultaneously fill the roles of dashing romantic adventurer and seriously devoted (maybe even borderline henpecked) fiancé. Buttercup first knows him as her subservient farmhand, and his response to her every request is, "As you wish." Every woman loves to have minions, of course, so having such an eager and handsome one tickles Buttercup's fancy no end. But Westley knows he's got to go make an independent person of himself before they marry, else he'll never have his love's true respect. So off he goes and doesn't come back until he's a world-renowned man of action. Buttercup can't believe that this self-possessed pillar of macho resolve is her farm boy—until she realizes that he will *still* do anything she wishes. To have the power of another entire human being at your disposal: that's an overwhelming gift for one person to give to another, and if trust and respect are to flourish, it demands utter reciprocation. Otherwise, you end up with a power imbalance that can't be sustained—just look at Ann Darrow and poor King Kong. But Buttercup and Westley *had* that kind of mutually trusting relationship, and that's ultimately what made it, famously, "true love."

III.
WE ARE
ALL INDIVIDUALS

(WISDOM ABOUT HUMANKIND)

"KNEEL BEFORE ZOD!"

—GENERAL ZOD, *SUPERMAN*

"CRIMINALS ARE A SUPERSTITIOUS, COWARDLY LOT."

—BATMAN, *DETECTIVE COMICS*

LET'S FACE IT: The thing about villains is that we all hear the call. We all, eventually, reach that point where we'd like to cut loose and tell the world what to go do with itself. The villains are the ones who get to do all the cool stuff: dream up ingenious plans, show off superweapons, and command minions to fight and die on their behalf. More to the point, good villains are the ones determined to be the protagonists in a story of their own devising. Their actions motivate the hero, their intelligence drives the plot, their declarations make the world dance to their tune. Or so they think. But there's a catch: What looks like strength really isn't. Villains are people too weak to master their own interactions with the world, so they're determined to hand off their problems to everyone else. In fact, it doesn't take bravery to steal from another; it doesn't take balls to mess with someone else's life. Doing these things is easy. Those who succumb to the lure, who can't commit to accomplishing the truly difficult—learning to weave their own thread into life's pattern rather than tearing a hole through the bits they don't like—take the coward's way. And for this, they live a life of unease. They see enemies in every shadow, because human beings are predisposed to see ourselves in others. The casual racist assumes others are equally small-minded. The white-collar criminal thinks everyone else is gaming the system, too. And the common street criminal, low man on the totem pole of wickedness? He assumes everyone else is out to get him, just as he is out to get others. If you've ever done something you knew was wrong, no matter how small, you've taken a taste of how the villain lives every day. Yet any person, no matter their status or place in society, need only assert responsibility for their own fate to rise above the gutter. Bravery is in living well regardless of your circumstances.

Batman's scorn for criminals was articulated in his very first story: *Detective Comics* #27 (1939).

"IT'S PEOPLE. SOYLENT GREEN IS MADE OUT OF PEOPLE."

—DETECTIVE THORN, *SOYLENT GREEN*

WHEN CHARLTON HESTON'S THORN makes this dire proclamation at the close of 1973's *Soylent Green*, the ramifications of what he's uncovered become clear: In a world stricken with ever-scarcer resources and an ever-growing population, the bodies of the recently dead are being processed into the wafers that serve as the food supply for the citizenry—a necessary evil for the world to continue on its path without a care for the consequences of our consumption. It's the ultimate expression of dystopic paranoia, and the truly frightening part is that it's not too far removed from the age we're living in right now. That doesn't mean you need to give that potato chip you're about to eat a closer look in case it's actually the remains of your buddy. But perhaps you should consider how, whether children in sweatshops or migrants working under substandard conditions, the lifestyle of comfort that we likely take for granted has been built on a foundation of systemic dehumanization. It's made out of people.

The climactic revelation of *Soylent Green* might be considered a spoiler, but it was seared indelibly into the public consciousness by a hilarious parody from Phil Hartman on *Saturday Night Live* in the late 1980s.

"IDEAS ARE BULLETPROOF."

—V, *V FOR VENDETTA*

I F THERE'S ONE THING Alan Moore is good at, it's anarchist characters who get to the heart of the matter. (And then perish.) In *V for Vendetta* both the principled cause and the willingness to die for it are necessary to effect change in a totalitarian regime. Though one hopes that our own society hasn't quite reached that point, there's certainly no shortage of legitimate threats today to freedom of ideas. The Internet, the closest thing we have to an utterly free exchange of information, is under so much threat of censorship—from both governments and tele-communications companies—that hacking around institutional firewalls has become a cottage industry. However, it's individuals' privacy that's coming under real fire. Bloggers are harassed for breaking controversial stories, and Facebook, one of the most ubiquitous social networks on the planet, has become little more than that guy who sits in the bushes outside your house. Ideas are bulletproof, yes, but they're only as strong as the protections granted to those exercising them.

Cory Doctorow, one of our generation's übergeeks, achieved that status by simultaneously undertaking one career as a science-fiction novelist and another as an Internet-rights activist with the Electronic Frontier Foundation.

"THERE ARE 10 KINDS OF PEOPLE IN THE WORLD: THOSE WHO UNDERSTAND BINARY, AND THOSE WHO DON'T."

—THINKGEEK T-SHIRT

IF YOU'D NEVER heard of the digits 2 through 9, you could still count from 0 to 10, you'd just have to write the numbers differently: 0, 1, 10, 11, 100, 101, 110, 111, 1000, 1001, 1010. That's how a computer does it, in the harsh, unflinching 1-0/on-off/ yes-no of binary nota- tion, and that's why com- puter-science nerds find this T-shirt hilarious—the "10" actually means "two." Rarely has an epigraph engaged in such vigorous dialogue with its own subtext. On the one hand, it's incredibly self-reinforcing: *There are only two kinds of people in the world—us, who perceive the world correctly in strict, black-and-white, binary opposition, and them, who don't.* You can practically hear the dogma giving itself a high five. But the spirit lurking a bit deeper beneath the sentiment sings a different tune: *There are alternate ways to see the world that reveal hidden possibilities.* Surely, if there can be one alternative to common wisdom on something as fundamental to life as numbers, it's not much of a leap to realize there's probably another, and another, and another. Heck, that holds true even in computer science itself; just ask the thousands—excuse me, the 3E8s—of people who laugh at binary while figuring in hexadecimal.

ThinkGeek.com sells this T-shirt. May all the gods bless ThinkGeek. Who else brings us a plush killer rabbit from *Monty Python*, canned unicorn meat, and a TARDIS USB hub, all at the same online store?

"MR. AND MRS. DURSLEY, OF NUMBER FOUR PRIVET DRIVE, WERE PROUD TO SAY THAT THEY WERE PERFECTLY NORMAL, THANK YOU VERY MUCH."

—J. K. ROWLING, *HARRY POTTER AND THE PHILOSOPHER'S STONE*

AHHH . . . GOOD OLD "NORMAL." It's an idea that clings to us with bewildering tenacity. The implication is that there's a baseline human standard of everythingness that represents how we "should" live—yet half a second of considering what life on earth truly looks like shows that, of course, that's not true. Still, note that Mr. and Mrs. Dursley were pointedly proud to be normal, proud not to be noticed, proud not to be special. Oh, my! Geeks understand that spending your time trying to "act normal" is a special kind of hell. Not because we want to be different just for the sake of being different—that's as bad as militant normalcy, if not worse—but because, in the end, happiness means accepting who you are, even if it turns out that who you are involves standing out like a tattooed, costumed, dice-rolling, blue-haired sore thumb. And because, well, normal is a fantasy far more ridiculous than a secret school of wizards. Nobody's normal—and those who insist they are *are broken people.*

Harry Potter and the Philosopher's Stone was published in 1997. The seven-novel series that ensued soon became the publishing phenomenon of the century, encouraging millions of children worldwide not to worry so much about being "normal."

"THE CAKE IS A LIE."

— *PORTAL*

GLaDOS, THE ARTIFICIAL INTELLIGENCE who serves as the primary antagonist in Valve's critically acclaimed video game, possesses a rare and unexpected trait for a computer. She lies. When she tells you, "There will be cake," what she really means is there will be death. But hey, doesn't cake sound a lot better? This hypothetical serving of nonexistent dessert is *Portal*'s understated way of symbolizing the lies told to us in any oppressive and deceitful system. The cake is the promise of safety from enemies that's used to excuse intrusive government policies. It is the "I love you; I promise it won't happen again" of the abusive spouse. It is the advertisement for terrific new stuff to buy that will surely make tomorrow happier than today. We've all been offered the cake. Some of us, the hundredth or thousandth times we've reached for the cake, have noticed what's actually being served on our plates and have tried to tell people what we've seen. The trouble is getting them to listen. Because, well, who doesn't like cake?

Portal (2007) is the first true science-fiction classic written in the medium of video games. If you've played it, you know this. If you haven't, go play it.

"THE SPICE MUST FLOW."

—DUNE

ECONOMIC SYSTEMS are bigger than people. That's why distribution of the precious mind-expanding spice, mélange, that is the lifeblood of galactic society in Frank Herbert's *Dune* must continue unimpeded. That's why, when Paul Atreides—the young nobleman who finds himself hailed as a prophesied savior—asserts his messianic will over the hitherto-powerless throngs of poor wretches living amid the spice mines of Arrakis, he causes commerce to grind to a standstill across a thousand planets, bringing the entire universe to heel. Just as the spice is Herbert's thinly veiled stand-in for oil, gold, or any commodity that greases the wheels of earthly progress, its necessity highlights the inherent danger of linking *any* one such commodity with the maintenance of a particular status quo—whether cheap gas for our cars or cheap clothes at Wal-Mart. "He who controls the spice controls the universe," says the evil Baron Harkonnen elsewhere in Herbert's epic, and it's a lesson that Paul takes to heart, bringing an entire monolithic structure of ingrained corruption down on the heads of those whose only real job was maintaining it. Economic systems are bigger than people . . . except when they're not.

The *Dune* saga becomes extremely amusing if you imagine that the spice was, in fact, coffee.

"FACTS DO NOT CEASE TO EXIST BECAUSE THEY ARE IGNORED."

—ALDOUS HUXLEY

HUMAN BEINGS are very good at ignoring reality. We've had renaissances and ages of reason, but even at our most rational we are a superstitious, irrational species. We are set in our ways. We too often celebrate outmoded ideals and cling to ways of doing things that have long since been revealed as pointless or even detrimental. Even when there's overwhelming evidence that our sincere intentions lead to more harm than good—for a perfect example, just look back at Prohibition in America—we do our best to pretend otherwise and repeat those same mistakes. Maybe it's a collective inability to admit when we're wrong, and we're all just exhibiting the stubborn pride of the know-it-all writ large. Maybe despite what we tell ourselves, we remain an emotional species rather than a rational species. One thing is clear, though: Facts are our friends. The longer we as a society insist on ignoring them when they get too uncomfortable, the more we erode our potential to be truly great.

Aldous Huxley's 1932 novel *Brave New World* was an early science-fiction classic that endures as high school recommended reading. But his most fundamental geek truism, quoted here, is from his essay collection *Proper Studies* (1927).

"THE WORLD IS ONLY BROKEN INTO TWO TRIBES: THE PEOPLE WHO ARE ASSHOLES AND THE PEOPLE WHO ARE NOT."

—SHERMAN ALEXIE, *THE ABSOLUTELY TRUE DIARY OF A PART-TIME INDIAN*

SOMEHOW, GEEKS ARE ASSHOLE MAGNETS. There's something about being sincerely attached to a nonmainstream pursuit that traditionally brings the jerks out of the woodwork sniffing for scapegoats. Often these same assholes are avid fans of something themselves and just can't make the connection that one man's fantasy sports team is another man's online RPG. Luckily, the Internet's ability to connect geeks has given us a community that helps combat our tendency toward solitude. That's not to say that geeks can't be assholes to one another, too. Racism, for instance. Consider the assholishness on display with many publishers' continued practice of taking books starring black characters and giving them covers that depict those characters as white, because "it'll sell better that way." Sure, and buses were better organized when African Americans had to sit in the back. Here's hoping we speed up the process of dealing with such questions, because it behooves all of us to work toward a better understanding of one another. We have enough trouble with outside assholes to be dealing with ones of our own.

The "whitewashed" cover-art issue blew up in 2009, when author Justine Larbalestier found that the African American tomboy protagonist of her novel *Liar* had been pictured as a white girl on the cover of the U.S. edition.

"THERE ARE WEAPONS THAT ARE SIMPLY THOUGHTS. FOR THE RECORD, PREJUDICES CAN KILL AND SUSPICION CAN DESTROY."

—ROD SERLING, *THE TWILIGHT ZONE*,
"THE MONSTERS ARE DUE ON MAPLE STREET"

THIS CLASSIC *TWILIGHT ZONE* EPISODE hinges on an alien invasion that employs human beings' own fear and distrust of one another—easy to arouse, even easier to enflame—to turn an otherwise ordinary neighborhood against itself and do the invaders' job for them. As he did so often from his *Twilight Zone* pulpit, Serling uses the epigraph above to express frustration with an unfortunate reality of the human condition. The essential truth at the heart of Serling's dark fable is equally applicable regardless of which "other" we choose to point our finger at; it has manifested at least enough times to allow Japanese Americans to be herded into camps for fear that they were the "enemy" and for countless law-abiding citizens to lose their livelihoods after being labeled Communists during the Red Scare.

The wisdom of Serling's sentiment makes it easy to see why "Maple Street" was crowned the all-time best episode of the series by *Time* magazine. Like all great science fiction, it succeeds by pointedly asking its audience: "What would you do?"

Some of the greatest science-fiction writers of the century contributed stories to *The Twilight Zone*: Ray Bradbury, Richard Matheson, Jerome Bixby. This one was written by series creator Serling himself.

"LIFE'S A BITCH. NOW SO AM I."

—CATWOMAN, *BATMAN RETURNS*

RARELY HAS THERE BEEN so loaded a feminist statement in the middle of the boy's club comic-movie genre. When Selina Kyle delivers it, she's just thwarted her boss's attempt to murder her, trashed all the trappings of her traditionally feminine home, and violently constructed a threatening new identity. And yet: That identity involves a skintight leather catsuit and a full face of makeup, which doesn't scream "empowered, outspoken feminist" so much as it does "dominatrix wet dream of a million teenagers." What's more, Catwoman is hardly a bitch; she strikes out against her enemies, sure, but that's no bitchier than any stunt the Penguin pulls. This two-faced social construct—of angry woman as vengeful bitch, and of angry woman as secretly lusty sex object—is a common and problematic one. In the film, though, director Tim Burton gives a nod to the cinematic tradition of cheesecake femmes fatales while taking care to show us the tormented individual behind the mask. We can only hope that general perceptions will shift similarly, so when we look at a woman—angry or not, sexy or not—we see a person rather than a stereotype.

Catwoman has been played by a different actor every year she's been adapted into film and television. Michelle Pfeifer was as different from Eartha Kitt as Halle Berry was from Julie Newmar. Still, the character endures.

"THANK YOU, MARIO! BUT OUR PRINCESS IS IN ANOTHER CASTLE!"

— SUPER MARIO BROS.

IF PINT-SIZE PLUMBER Mario is anything, he's persistent. Time and again he trudges through strange lands peopled with creatures out to get him, and time and again he appears to have accomplished his goal only to have the rug pulled out from under him. Mario might as well be a blue collar guy trying to get through the workweek. For him the end of the week isn't the end, it's just a brief pause before setting off for the next castle, chasing a princess he'll never rescue because the game is designed to keep her perpetually out of reach. Yet Mario doesn't seem to mind. He doesn't even appear to notice. Neither do the Marios of the real world. They chase their princesses, navigating pipes and pitfalls and creatures only to find she's always in the next castle. The cycle is unbreakable. And so we've got to ask, is Mario depressingly oblivious to his circumstances, or is he the admirable embodiment of working-class perseverance? And is there even a difference?

Mario was first introduced as the hero of *Donkey Kong* in 1981, at which time he was called "Jumpman." Because, you know, he jumped. He only got his name the following year in *Donkey Kong Junior,* the only game in which he's been depicted as the villain.

"LISTEN TO THEM. CHILDREN OF THE NIGHT. WHAT MUSIC THEY MAKE."

—DRACULA (1931)

DRACULA'S WISTFUL INTERJECTION has long been the rallying cry of goths worldwide; there's something about the reverential way Dracula mentioned the wolves outside his door that speaks to the heart of every geek who's ever been well acquainted with the night. Among geeks, goths are often a breed unto themselves, situated between horror fans and theater nerds. Goths are aesthetically oriented and have a seemingly endless appetite for dark-spun fairy tales and other subtle horrors. They also have the honor of being some of the most misunderstood of all geek-kind by those who don't seem to grasp the difference between a role-playing goth and an actual vampire. (It takes all kinds, we guess.) However, most goths are able to shake it off and revel in one of geekdom's earnest and most active communities, where they can mingle with others who sincerely share their passions. Bonus: The goth music scene is pretty killer, so even the casual-geek passerby can find out just what music they *do* make.

A lot of kids in today's steampunk scene used to identify with the goth aesthetic—and are pleasantly surprised to discover that normal adults seem intrigued, rather than alarmed, by this new thing. Well, *yeah*. People think of goths as weirdoes who take vampires too seriously, and therefore they can't help being worried on some level that a crazy goth might, you know, want to make them bleed. Whereas steampunks are—what? Weirdoes who take pocket watches too seriously? What are they gonna do, vehemently tell you what time it is?

"THE TRUTH IS OUT THERE."

—FOX MULDER, *THE X-FILES*

PROFESSIONAL INVESTIGATORS: detectives, reporters, intelligence agents. They're incredibly important to us, both in reality and in our belief structures, because we know we've gotta be able to rely on *someone* to uncover the nasty little secrets the world is keeping from us. Specific investigative types have come in and out of vogue over the years; for example, it's not au courant to trust reporters these days, because large numbers of shitty ones on television have dragged down the standard by which we measure them all. But there will always be hidden truths, and there will always be people who are determined to shine a light on them. The trick is figuring out: Which of these seekers after revelation are really interested in helping you understand what matters *to you*? Because we've all got our agendas, and there's no definitive guide to them. That fact—not men-in-black conspiracies—is what makes the truth so darn hard to sort out.

Mulder was great, but our favorite TV journalist remains Jack McGee from *The Incredible Hulk*. In the beginning, he was just after a scoop that would make a great story; by the end of his pursuit, he was deeply invested in uncovering the truth, no matter *how* far out there.

"I'M NOT ANTI-SOCIAL, I'M JUST NOT USER-FRIENDLY."

—T-SHIRT

LOOK, SOME PEOPLE JUST SUCK. Most geeks grow up enough on the fringes to be able to identify a problem crowd when they see one. Those same geeks have gotten pretty good at entertaining themselves. The combination can often result in a group of people with common life experiences enjoying themselves together—and a geek sitting nearby, frowning at their dance moves and tweeting furiously. Dear non-geeks: If you see any geeks wearing this shirt in public, they have come from a long day at the IT mines trying to explain to people how to double-click on something. Leave them be. And to be fair: Dear geeks, We understand where you're coming from, but every once in a while, if you look closely, there will be someone in the crowd with whom you have something awesome in common. (Hint: +1 for anyone not dancing the Macarena.) Don't be any more alienated than you really need to be.

Only in the tech world can you call someone a "user" and not mean it as a put-down.

"I LOVED IT. IT WAS MUCH BETTER THAN *CATS*. I'M GOING TO SEE IT AGAIN AND AGAIN."

—HYPNOTIZED THEATERGOERS, *SATURDAY NIGHT LIVE*

FOR THOSE OF US whose interests lie outside the mainstream—and if you're reading this book, yours almost certainly do—most of the people who consume a steady diet of American mass-media culture might as well be hypnotized, droning on and on about how much they like the latest bit of predictable blandness that passes for entertainment in the twenty-first century. Even as we yearn for something better, something smarter, something that engages muscles in our brains and souls we haven't flexed before, we see our neighbors doing little more than repeating what they've heard others saying. *The Truly Real Superstar Babysitters of Orange County*? They loved it. It was much better than whatever was cool last month. They're going to see it again and again. And they really will, because mass culture is built to frown upon anything that isn't conformity. Meanwhile, one thing that has always separated the geek from the pack is that the geek scoffs at conformity. Rest assured, we didn't love it. We're not going to see it again and again. And we like it that way.

Though the quote endures, not many people remember that the "it" referred to was a performance by the hypnotist known as "The Amazing Alexander," portrayed by Jon Lovitz (1986). We think that counts as irony.

"I CAN HAS CHEEZBURGER?"

—INTERNET MEME

TAKE TWO NEWS STORIES. One is a horrible crime, maybe a double murder. Throw in some arson for good measure. The other involves a YouTube video of an adorable kitten being slapped by a thoughtless teenager. Two dead people and a burned-down house later, there will be ten, twenty, a hundred times more outrage about the slapped kitten. The fact is, we recognize ourselves for the really smart yet often cruel apes we are—and are drawn to what we see as innocence in our cats and dogs. One might call that self-loathing, but it's more than that. It's a manifestation of our sense of justice. Humans are victims? Sad, but then, people suck. Kittens are victims? Utterly outrageous! Grab the pitchforks! So when a cheeseburger-loving cat spawned an Internet explosion of grammar-impaired cat pictures, geek culture was doing more than having a laugh. It was putting its protective arms around the very embodiment of the innocence we as a species lack.

While icanhascheezburger.com has become a time-tested favorite, let's not forget that it all started in 2007 at somethingawful.com.

"*LIKE* AND *EQUAL* ARE NOT THE SAME THING AT ALL."

—MEG MURRY, *A WRINKLE IN TIME*

O N THE DISTANT PLANET CAMAZOTZ, human-like aliens are ruled by an authoritarian dictator in the form of a giant, pulsating brain that mentally directs all their actions. Visiting Earth girl Meg Murry discovers this horrific state of affairs when she sees all the kids who live on a Camazotzian suburban block step out of their homes simultaneously and start bouncing their balls in unison—a form of "play" that looks more like the children are mere flesh-colored pistons pumping away in a big machine. In this one freaky image, Madeleine L'Engle made crystal clear the difference between fascism and progressive democracy—a difference that the argumentative rhetoric of today's political pundits, sadly, has sometimes sought to obfuscate. The "all men are created equal" that is the basis of American civil rights doesn't mean we think our lives should all follow the same paths. What it means is that no one else can claim a right to take away our shoes and hobble us along the way.

A Swiftly Tilting Planet, the second sequel to *A Wrinkle in Time*, prefigured the basic premise of the sci-fi television classic *Quantum Leap*—the hero entering the body of a person in the past to set right a glitch in destiny—by a full decade.

"A CONCLUSION IS THE PLACE WHERE YOU GOT TIRED OF THINKING."

—STEVEN WRIGHT

BEING A GEEK can be mentally exhausting; we totally get it. However, the collective short attention span we've inherited from the Internet age means that it's all too easy to answer a pressing question by glancing at Wikipedia and calling it a day. Occasionally that's all you need; it doesn't take too many sources to corroborate the orbital period of Venus, for example. On the other hand, it seems vaguely disheartening that, with access to more information than ever before, so many Internet fights boil down to two people with violently opposing viewpoints attacking each other based on incorrect and incomplete data sets. It's our responsibility as geeks to make sure we never stop learning, that we take little for granted, and that we look at every statement not as a conclusion, but as an invitation to more research.

For all his geek cred, standup comedian Steven Wright has only one clear-cut geek-themed performance to his credit: the 2005 comic-book movie *Son of the Mask*.

"WE'RE ALL MAD HERE."

—ALICE'S ADVENTURES IN WONDERLAND

FEW LITERARY HEROES have the universal, all-ages appeal of Lewis Carroll's rabbit-hole-investigating young miss. In her day, she's been held up as a model of whimsical childhood, as a surrealist pioneer, as an extended metaphor for the society of her contemporaries. (There really is something about a dodo race that's so very open to interpretation.) However, throughout the myriad adaptations of this iconic tale, its core has remained intact: a world that makes no sense, and a girl who's stuck in it with no way out. It's a telling arc, quite different from many of the other coming-of-age stories that pit their young protagonist against an evil that can be defeated. Alice is more world-weary than that,

and it's that perspective—the misunderstood, often-frustrated outsider—that makes her such a hero in the lit-geek circle. Because let's face it: Sometimes the only way to face the world is to go a little mad.

Alice's Adventures in Wonderland (note the proper title) was published in 1865; the sequel, *Through the Looking-Glass, and What Alice Found There*, in 1871.

"THERE'S JUST SOMETHING ABOUT AN ANATOMICALLY CORRECT RUBBER SUIT THAT PUTS FIRE IN A GIRL'S LIPS."

—POISON IVY, *BATMAN AND ROBIN*

THERE ARE TWO WAYS to look at Batman. For the past decade or so, pop culture has approached him as the down-and-dirty antihero whose Gotham City is a gritty chaos. This interpretation was a pretty direct backlash against the 1997 movie *Batman and Robin*, which had more color than a box of Crayola and all the dramatic tension of a blooper reel. However, Batman's always been as much high camp as high -noir, even when the line between the self-referential and the markedly unaware is thin. Believe it or not, this offers a valuable lesson: Multiple readings of a text can be equally valid—a fact that can be easy to forget in an era when Internet comment sections often read like the transcript of the weekly debate of the Extremists' Society.* Some interpretations might be less successful, which this movie outing certainly was, but just disliking an interpretation doesn't invalidate it. Worth remembering, the next time you encounter someone who's wrong on the Internet. (There's also a second lesson to be found in this quote: Don't wear an anatomically correct rubber suit unless you want to put fire in a girl's lips. More specific, but equally handy.)

---

*This is a joke. There is no such thing as the Extremists' Society. And if you disagree, you are a Nazi who should die in a fire.

"THERE'S NO CRYING IN BASEBALL!"

—JIMMY DUGAN, *A LEAGUE OF THEIR OWN*

SOME GENERALIZATIONS are just more immortal than others. When reluctant Girls' League coach Jimmy Dugan berates weeping right-fielder Evelyn with this gem, it's both hilarious and patently untrue—I mean, sports were basically invented so men can fight one another and then cry, right? In context, the tirade says more about Dugan's still-lingering misogyny than anything else. However, it's been neatly co-opted by geeks, and as such has become a go-to response for anyone that's taking something too much to heart. It's equally untrue every time (if something's worth caring about, someone has cried over it), but there's a *je ne sais quoi* about the vast and epic sweep of the generalization involved that's reclaimed this phrase to be almost encouraging—the sort of suck-it-up advice one gives to a fellow soldier in the trenches. So geeks, keep on caring enough to cry, even when people tell you there's no crying in . . . well, anything.

Things in which there definitely is crying include comic books, *Star Trek*, *Buffy the Vampire Slayer*, and, of course, *I Love Lucy*.

"I WILL NOT BE PUSHED, FILED, STAMPED, INDEXED, BRIEFED, DEBRIEFED, OR NUMBERED. MY LIFE IS MY OWN."

—NUMBER SIX, *THE PRISONER*

WHEN PATRICK MCGOOHAN'S Number Six angrily defies his captors with this litany in the seminal British secret-agent series' opening installment, he crystallizes everything we need to know about the battle of ideas, ideology, and identity that spans the show's all-too brief run. The premise, featuring the dogged, dogmatic Six bedeviled at every turn in his attempts to escape from mysterious captors and reclaim his identity, hinges on the idea that we're all boxed in by a system—whatever that system is—that controls us at every step, and any notions of breaking free from that box are themselves just one more level of control. This makes for one big puzzle of positively Kafka-esque proportions. Although *The Prisoner* goes to great lengths to hold any definitive answers at arm's length, the mere fact that McGoohan's character clings so desperately to his individualism, yet is never more than a number to us, is ample testament to the ultimate futility of his struggle.

The free-will-versus-determinism debate embodied by Number Six in *The Prisoner* (1967) also lies at the heart of the character of the Cylon Number Six in *Battlestar Galactica* (2005). Coincidence? We think not.

"SO IT GOES."

—KURT VONNEGUT, *SLAUGHTERHOUSE-FIVE*

STRANGE AS IT SOUNDS, the most disturbing and tragic part of Kurt Vonnegut's meditation on war, inhumanity, and suffering isn't the violence and horror he shows us, it's the impassionate distance at which the narrator puts himself from it all. Men are born. They suffer. They slaughter one another before dying themselves, often horribly, often at the hands of another human being. So it goes. If we can embrace such coldness, are we then empty shells or are we merely protecting our psyche from deep emotional damage? Cynical as Vonnegut was, it's nice to think he wanted us to take away the latter rather than the former. We can neither take part in the horror of man's violence nor give in to it, but we *must* acknowledge it. In some way we must come to grips with what we're capable of doing to one another. We are a beautiful, terrible, sleepless species. And sometimes we're still animals. So it goes.

Slaughterhouse-Five (1969) is often grouped with several other geek novels from the 1950s and '60s: Ray Bradbury's *Fahrenheit 451* and Joseph Heller's *Catch-22*. Lesson: Brainy satire and titles with numbers work well together.

"SPECIALIZATION IS FOR INSECTS."

—ROBERT HEINLEIN, *TIME ENOUGH FOR LOVE*

THINK ABOUT your favorite handheld device. Dollars to donuts says it doesn't just serve as a phone, or a camera, or an automatic coffee stirrer. It probably does a whole bunch of these things. You love it for that very reason. After all, if electronics are capable of doing so many incredible things, why shouldn't one device be able to handle them all? Robert Heinlein thought the  same should apply to human beings—and he was right. Heinlein was a boot-strappy Libertarian amid liberal peers decades before it became trendy, and he took his fair share of criticism for those stringent beliefs. But one thing he can't be accused of is underestimating the human ability to achieve. Excel at many things, he told us. Be capable. Be adept. Be smart and strong and focused. That is our mandate as human beings, and Heinlein's stories are littered with people who show us how. We can say what we will about his views on, say, war, but few can argue against aspiring to be a well-rounded, multitalented person. So go forth and learn how to fix a bicycle, and how to understand ancient history, and how to vacuum corners, and how to calculate a number sequence. You'll be happier.

The rest of the quote from *Time Enough for Love* (1973) is long but worth memorizing: "A human being should be able to change a diaper, plan an invasion, butcher a hog, conn a ship, design a building, write a sonnet, balance accounts, build a wall, set a bone, comfort the dying, take orders, give orders, cooperate, act alone, solve equations, analyze a new problem, pitch manure, program a computer, cook a tasty meal, fight efficiently, die gallantly."

"I HAVE ANOTHER TRICK FOR YOU. WANNA SEE ME MAKE ALL THE WHITE PEOPLE DISAPPEAR?"

—THE CARD TRICKSTER, *THE BROTHER FROM ANOTHER PLANET*

JOHN SAYLES'S 1984 FILM features an eponymous protagonist: a gawky, mute alien who coincidentally happens to resemble a black man. In very short order, it was embraced by non-white geeks as a cutting-edge classic, a perfect parable of race in geekdom. There's a central dilemma they deal with: Because most geeks have, historically speaking, generally identified as outcasts on the margins of society, they often have trouble understanding that it's possible for some geeks to be marginalized even within geekdom due to other qualities of identity, such as gender, race, and class. The Brother of Sayles's movie struggles to find his place in the surreal and blighted landscape of 1980s New York—specifically, Harlem. He has almost nothing in common with his fellow Harlemites but the color of his skin. Yet in a society so powerfully impacted by race, skin color is more than enough to forge a common bond.

The titular Brother was portrayed by Joe Morton, who would later achieve further geek cred as Dr. Steven Hamilton on *Smallville* and the guy who destroyed the future in *Terminator 2*.

"MONSTERS, JOHN!
MONSTERS FROM THE ID!"

—LT. "DOC" OSTROW, FORBIDDEN PLANET

MORE THAN ANCIENT squid creatures from another dimension, atomic-powered giant insects, and chain-saw-wielding zombies with frickin' laser beams attached to their heads, we fear that which is in ourselves. Humanity's ties to our primitive past are not as distant as we'd like to believe, and in our hearts we know it. Our darkest thoughts, wants, desires—these things are a terror far greater than any monster we could conjure, not simply because they're so difficult to confront, but because they show that we're a mere half-step removed from the animals. Worse still, our minds are fragile things. Barely controllable. If we were to lose control? We fear we'd cease to be human, because more than any amount of spirituality, faith, or technical know-how, it is our conscience, self-awareness, and desire to rise above our primitive roots that is the soul of man. If we retreat to the id—our unconscious, instinctual mind—we abandon all that separates us from the apes. And that is the most frightening thing imaginable.

Freud introduced the concept of the id in his 1920 essay "Beyond the Pleasure Principle." *Forbidden Planet*, the greatest science-fiction film ever inspired by Shakespeare, explored the id more tangibly in 1956.

"ONLY SPARTAN WOMEN GIVE BIRTH TO REAL MEN."

—QUEEN GORGO, *300*

"THE ANALYTICAL ENGINE WEAVES ALGEBRAIC PATTERNS, JUST AS THE JACQUARD LOOM WEAVES FLOWERS AND LEAVES."

—ADA LOVELACE, ON CHARLES BABBAGE'S ANALYTICAL ENGINE

THE REAL QUEEN GORGO of Sparta was a political mover and shaker on par with the modern age's most respected power brokers. She was also a geek and early cryptanalyst, helping her fellow Spartans find the code hidden in a chiseled wooden board that warned of impending Persian attack. And, predictably, she may also have been one of the first targets of geek sexism, for she is lauded in many historians' accounts not for her own (substantial) accomplishments, but primarily for her relationship to the men around her—as the daughter, wife, and mother of kings. But while Gorgo's quote in Frank Miller's *300* is a fairly accurate rendering of her words as recorded by Plutarch, the true context was quite different. Per Plutarch, Gorgo didn't use the word *real*—and she was speaking to a woman from Attica who asked her how Spartan women had gained the power to rule Spartan men. Placed in this female-to-female context, Gorgo's declaration becomes less a statement on her value in the eyes of men and more subversive—perhaps an encouragement from one woman to another on methods of escaping oppression and gaining power of her own. Gorgo may also have been implying that men can be partners in this process, if they are willing . . . or pawns, shaped from birth by the power of maternal influence, if not.

Nineteenth-century writer Ada Lovelace may be one of the first women to triumph over the historical biases against Queen Gorgo. Though in her lifetime she was most known as the poet Byron's daughter, today she's remembered as the world's first computer programmer.

"OUT OF MY WAY.
I'M GOING TO SEE MY MOTHER."

—SEPHIROTH, *FINAL FANTASY VII*

SEPHIROTH: BADASS. Super-soldier. Terrifying megalo-maniacal mass-murdering sociopath . . . and mama's boy. An entire generation of geeks was transformed by *Final Fantasy VII*, for reasons that had little to do with the game's groundbreaking graphics or gameplay. Games with complex plots and three-dimensional characters had been popular in Japan for some time, but *Final Fantasy VII* was the first introduction for many American gamers to the concept of games as an art form—as truly interactive storytelling. What made it work was the way so many of the characters resonated as their facets were gradually revealed. True, none of us were stereotypical fantasy-story warriors able to wield gigantic swords or summon dragons, as the game's hero Cloud appeared at first glance. But all of us could understand the kind of crippling insecurity that lurked behind Cloud's stoic facade. Most of us had no great desire to dominate the earth, but we all knew what it was to struggle for the approval of a parent or authority figure. Even if that parent was an incomprehensible alien life form—or the real-world equivalent thereof.

Final Fantasy VII was released in 1997—a decade into the series' life. The saga continues today: *Final Fantasy XIV* debuted in 2010.

"WHAT IS YOUR DAMAGE, HEATHER?"

—HEATHERS

YOU KNOW WHAT'S THE WORST? High school. Every geek has seen the havoc high school can wreak, in a way few mainstreamers can understand. Somehow, most teen movies construct their stories so that their heroine ends up with the dream date at the school dance, their hero wins the big game, and everything ends up all right. But most of high school is not all right, and *Heathers* realized that. Head bitch Heather McNamara's signature catchphrase manages to be dismissive, aggressive, and superior at the same time—the soul-crushing gift of the high school cliquemaster—and literally haunts the counter-culture girl Veronica long after Heather is dead. Everyone who's been bullied recognizes the power play at work in this putdown; an important geek rite of passage to adulthood is trying to move past the power your too-cool enemies had over you. If you can't quite get there, well, we can hardly blame you—some meanness is immortal. As long as you don't start playing strip croquet with strangers, you'll probably be fine.

By starring in the quick triple threat of *Beetlejuice* (1988), *Heathers* (1989), and *Edward Scissorhands* (1990), Winona Ryder became the face of girl geekdom for a generation; it would continue with *Dracula*, *Little Women* (Jo is a protogeek!), and *Alien Resurrection*, among others.

"RAY, IF SOMEONE ASKS YOU IF YOU ARE A GOD, YOU SAY YES!"

—WINSTON ZEDDIMORE, *GHOSTBUSTERS*

"TELL HIM ABOUT THE TWINKIE."

—WINSTON ZEDDIMORE, *GHOSTBUSTERS*

GHOSTBUSTERS WAS, in its way, a straight-ahead satire of New York City. We laughed as much at the unflappability of the typical New Yorker as we did at the ridiculousness of the Stay-Puft Marshmallow Man. It wouldn't surprise us that any New Yorker might be so irreverent and arrogant as to claim godhood; in fact, many of us were surprised when Dan Aykroyd as Dr. Ray Stantz tried to deny it. *Ghostbusters* also poked fun at the arrogance of geeks. Ray and Egon, the brains of the outfit, might not have had the business acumen of Venkman or the earnestness of Winston, but they had this: *They were right.* The Twinkie comparison, the disaster of biblical proportions, the unlicensed particle accelerators; the whole thing was cockamamie, and it's a miracle any of them survived. But they knew their stuff and refused to back down from the importance of their knowledge, despite a city full of jaded naysayers. Because of their dogged insistence, the city was—more or less—prepared for a major disaster. So, when you get right down to it, Winston was right, too: After all that, a little bragging would have been completely apropos.

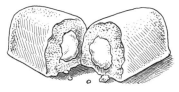

In the novelization of *Ghostbusters* (1984), we learn that Winston used to be a Marine; in the 1991 video-game sequel, it's revealed that he's a learned Egyptologist.

"WHY SO SERIOUS?"

—JOKER, *THE DARK KNIGHT*

BATMAN'S NEMESES over the years have rarely been superpowered; they were usually just a bit crueler and weirder than the norm. In earlier adaptations, the Joker was a Technicolor prankster who was more pun than prudence. After filmmaker Christopher Nolan's 2005 movie reboot, however, Batman's world was far darker, and it needed a Joker to match. The Joker of *The Dark Knight* as portrayed by Heath Ledger was a force of violent chaos, shocking even in the stakes-upping world of comic-movie sequels. Though superhero movies are nominally escapist fare, each iteration of Batman has reflected not just the Bat-world but the real world as well—which makes this Joker's rallying cry a bitter reminder that life today is just as messy as Gotham City, and that recent news headlines have featured quite

 a few criminals who could give the Joker a run for his money. It might be a stretch to say that the Joker is giving us a direct call to arms—but sometimes there's nothing wrong with taking stuff a little more seriously.

The Dark Knight (2008) was Heath Ledger's final complete performance before his untimely death at the age of twenty-eight.

"TRANSFORM AND ROLL OUT!"

—OPTIMUS PRIME, *THE TRANSFORMERS*

MORE THAN JUST A KICK-ASS CATCHPHRASE, the call to arms of Autobot leader Optimus Prime en route to impending battle with the evil Decepticons represents a philosophy that, when you cut it to the quick, isn't altogether different from what Martin Luther King Jr. was alluding to when he said: "Change does not roll in on the wheels of inevitability, but comes through continuous struggle." There's an underlying truth to the idea that one must enact change on the microcosmic level before attempting change on a global scale. And if there's anyone who nobly represented the dichotomy of both continuous struggle and the wheeling in of change, it was the Transformers. While Optimus and his robotic cohorts are perhaps overly literal exemplars of King's thesis, we take our wisdom where we find it. For an entire generation of children who came of age in the 1980s, that wisdom came from an animated robot who had a very deep voice, and who spent half his time disguised as a Mack truck.

In addition to playing Optimus Prime and Eeyore from *Winnie the Pooh*, voice actor Peter Cullen is the ear-catching basso whose narration has for decades heralded the introduction of countless action-movie trailers.

"YOU'RE TRAVELING THROUGH ANOTHER DIMENSION, A DIMENSION NOT ONLY OF SIGHT AND SOUND, BUT OF MIND."

—ROD SERLING, *THE TWILIGHT ZONE*

"I WAS BOLD IN THE PURSUIT OF KNOWLEDGE, NEVER FEARING TO FOLLOW TRUTH AND REASON TO WHATEVER RESULTS THEY LED, AND BEARDING EVERY AUTHORITY WHICH STOOD IN THEIR WAY."

—THOMAS JEFFERSON

THE WORLD is most often changed by ideas rather than by guns, bombs, and fists. Albert Einstein. Karl Marx. Thomas Jefferson. Carl Sagan. Men like these have sparked revolutions and given us new ways to see and understand our world. This is no surprise; geeks throughout history have long known the power of the mind. It wasn't until the twentieth century, however, that we developed a robust subculture that embraced the kind of flights of fancy that have come to define us. Jefferson correctly saw a need to fuel the mind, a cultural desire for speculation that gave people insight into the human condition. What he probably couldn't have imagined is how modern geek artists such as *The Twilight Zone*'s creative mastermind Rod Serling would take that same need, that same appreciation for the power of the mind, and apply the metaphorical trappings of surely frivolous juvenilia—talking dolls! space aliens!—to achieve pure entertainment *at the same time* as profound enlightenment. In their own way, the storytelling tropes that emerged from Serling's influence have been as sweeping a cultural revolution as anything Jefferson could have imagined.

Sometimes, geekery is of such high quality that it takes over mainstream culture. The Hollywood trade journal *Variety* called *The Twilight Zone* (1959) "the best that has ever been accomplished in half-hour filmed television."

"TO DOUBT EVERYTHING OR TO BELIEVE EVERYTHING ARE TWO EQUALLY CONVENIENT SOLUTIONS; BOTH DISPENSE WITH THE NEED FOR THOUGHT."

—HENRI POINCARÉ, *SCIENCE AND HYPOTHESIS*

WHETHER WE'RE TALKING about religious institutions or the news media, there are times when it's crucially important to doubt the information we're given and other times when the need to believe in *something* can be the only thing that offers any respite. Our tendency, however, is to choose one side or the other of that split and stay there. As human beings, we're fundamentally lazy. We don't like doing any more work than we have to or thinking any harder than we need to. That's at least partially to blame for the age of extreme partisan polarization we find ourselves in: Reason has been removed from the discussion, and it's become all about the ego we have invested in our point of view. What Poincaré points out, in addition to underscoring that inherent laziness, is how much more difficult it can be to navigate that razor's edge right down the middle. If we're ever to achieve true progress, it's concomitant to have both faith and doubt comforting us in equal measure.

French mathematician Poincaré (1854–1912) laid the groundwork for the modern fields of topology and chaos theory.

"ME FAIL ENGLISH? THAT'S UNPOSSIBLE!"

—RALPH WIGGUM, *THE SIMPSONS*

O N EVERY OTHER PAGE OF THIS BOOK, you will find us elaborating on the quotations above. On this page, you will not. Ralph's confused exclamation is like unto a Zen koan, and we suggest you meditate upon it. Then meditate upon it some more. We've been doing so for many years, and we still continue to find fresh nuances within.

We would like to humbly suggest that Ralph Wiggum, like Rose Nylund and Phoebe Buffay, is an avatar of Delirium of the Endless.

"MONKEYS' BRAINS, WHILE POPULAR IN CANTONESE CUISINE, ARE NOT OFTEN TO BE FOUND IN WASHINGTON, D.C."

—WADSWORTH, *CLUE*

THE WAY YOU SOLVE MYSTERIES is by identifying anomalies and tracking them to their source. In *Clue*, the ultimate parody of a murder mystery, everything was an anomaly; there was no baseline from which to deviate. That made the whole story an exercise in farce, but it also provided the opportunity for any number of complete-unto-themselves truisms. Here's one: you can't decipher a clue if you don't observe it. The above revelation was offered toward the end of the film by the Boddy mansion's butler, Wadsworth, as a key element in his chain of reasoning in solving the murder—but it's a total and deliberate cheat, as the very *fact* that monkeys' brains were the main course at dinner had never been mentioned. The line is emblematic of a narrative technique known formally in English masters' programs worldwide as "pulling something out of your ass." In a real mystery, that's against the rules; in a mystery parody, it's the source of humor; and in life, sometimes it's just what you gotta do. (Speaking of English classes. . . .)

Clue is a rarely cited credit of geek filmmaking icon John Landis (*The Blues Brothers*, *An American Werewolf in London*), who cowrote it with director Jonathan Lynn.

"YOU'RE A VAMPIRE. OH, I'M SORRY. WAS THAT AN OFFENSIVE TERM? SHOULD I SAY 'UNDEAD AMERICAN'?"

—BUFFY SUMMERS, *BUFFY THE VAMPIRE SLAYER*

BECAUSE SHE DOESN'T wear a skintight action suit, people sometimes miss the fact that Buffy Summers is, for all intents and purposes, a classic comic-book-style superhero. She exemplifies the life of every high-school girl—and, more than that, of every human being—writ on a larger, brighter canvas, the angst of her adolescent relationships exaggerated but not fundamentally changed by the fact that her daily routine puts her up against not just jerks and jocks but vampires and demons. This literalization of the metaphors of daily life stretches into the realm of identity politics when she sneers at her tormented vampire boyfriend, suggesting that perhaps his struggles will be less painful if the monstrous terminology of his existence is dressed up in politically correct language. Like Buffy, we've all caught ourselves on occasion saying snide, hurtful things to the ones we love—maybe even mocking or spurning something that matters profoundly to them. Yet beneath that moment of nastiness, Buffy can't forget that she found it in her heart to recognize and love Angel's damaged humanity in the first place. There's a lesson here for all of us: If you're going to breach the line of decorum, do it with someone you can trust to accept your apology later.

Writer Joss Whedon's snappy banter borrowed heavily from the flavor of Marvel Comics' trademark bickering on the battlefield, which is why fans cheered in 2004 to see him take up the pen to write Marvel's new Astonishing X-Men series.

IV.
KNOWING IS HALF THE BATTLE

(WISDOM ABOUT CONFLICT)

"HEY, YOU—GET YOUR DAMN HANDS OFF HER."

—GEORGE MCFLY, *BACK TO THE FUTURE*

I F YOU EVER DOUBT that there can be a lot going on in one sentence, take a look at George McFly: his utterance of these eight words ties together mistaken identity, sexual assault, burgeoning heroism, protoincest, and the twisting of the space-time continuum—and that's all before Biff even turns around. We all have instances in our lives in which it seems as though our many problems and dreams coalesce into a single, terrifying moment, and we know that how we decide to act in those crucial moments will change who we are. Oddly, George's true pivotal moment was making the decision to act at all; that inertia spilled over into real actions and real change. In the movie, it's a triumphant climax. In real life, making a tough decision at a crucial juncture often means that different troubles lie ahead. Yet the tough decision is often the right one, and it's always worth fighting a good fight.

Crispin Glover's portrayal of George McFly in *Back to the Future* (1985) was so memorable, it's hard to conceive anyone else having done it. That didn't stop the producers of the sequel from replacing him with an actor who accepted a lower salary.

"I FIND YOUR LACK OF FAITH DISTURBING."

—DARTH VADER, *STAR WARS*

ADMIRAL MOTTI thought he knew what he was dealing with. His boss, imperial high honcho Grand Moff Tarkin, had this right-hand man, Darth Vader, who got to do *whatever* he wanted *whenever* he wanted and was just *way* impressed with himself. Meanwhile, Motti, a good, hardworking soldier, spent a whole freaking decade wrangling the logistical nightmare of constructing a battle station the size of a freaking moon, only to be dismissed with a hand wave by this heavy-breathing asswipe. It's not hard to see that, after who knows how many management staff meetings where Vader doubtlessly kept mouthing off about "the power of the Force" this and "the power of the Force" that, Motti had had about enough and was ready to put Vader in his place. Here's where Motti went wrong: He misjudged his rival's moxie. He thought he knew the sort of response to expect after calling his coworker a douchebag. It never occurred to him that being maybe choked to death right there on the spot was even within the realm of possibility. So gauge your opponents correctly. How far will they go?

We would like to take this footnote to suggest that, the next time George Lucas goes back to mess with his films for another digitally altered version, perhaps he should replace all footage of the unmasked Anakin Skywalker with newly filmed and de-aged shots of James Earl Jones.

"GOOD DAY, SIR! . . . I SAID, GOOD DAY!"

—WILLY WONKA, *WILLY WONKA AND THE CHOCOLATE FACTORY*

JON STEWART has appropriated this huffy conversation-ending phrase in recent years, and though he always plays it for laughs, it really does epitomize in seven words the "extreme moderate" philosophy that fuels Stewart's appeal. See, when Willy Wonka hurls this dismissal at Charlie Bucket in response to Charlie's having broken the rules of the chocolate factory tour, he does so because he's angry—furious, in fact, that Charlie, for whom he had great hopes, has let him down. But he doesn't let his disappointed fury consume him. He doesn't call Charlie names. He simply expresses his anger . . . politely. His voice is loud and upset, but he keeps his words dignified. He quotes the contractual terms Charlie has violated, spells out the logical conclusion, and leaves it there. And by stopping short of the nuclear option, by being angry without becoming truly nasty, he thereby leaves an opening for Charlie to offer one more statement—which is exactly what it takes for the two to come back to the table and find a happy ending for their story. That distinction between forceful honesty and abuse is the line that Stewart—and the millions of Americans who love his show—wishes today's politicians would remember how to draw.

Chocolate Factory author Roald Dahl was a World War II flying ace who flew combat missions over Greece, was promoted to wing commander, and subsequently worked in British Intelligence alongside Ian Fleming.

"I HAVE COME HERE TO CHEW BUBBLEGUM AND KICK ASS, AND I'M ALL OUT OF BUBBLEGUM."

—THEY LIVE

R OWDY" RODDY PIPER'S LACK of bubblegum is not what prompted his alien ass-kicking spree. He had come to chew bubblegum *and* kick ass, after all. No "or" in the equation. If given the chance, he'd probably have been chewing that bubble gum *while* kicking alien ass, which is a lot more than most of us could hope to accomplish. Those goofy one-liners may be absurd, but they also say something about ourselves. It's like this: The wish fulfillment inherent in badass one-liners isn't merely about looking cool—it's about keeping your composure in situations that would make most of us curl up into the fetal position and cry. The ordinary-man-turned-hero is a mainstay of geek entertainment, yes, but we return to the witty tough guy for a reason. As much as we dream of overcoming great adversity and being a hero, what we really want is to do it without pissing our pants. So pass the bubblegum, please.

In 2010, acclaimed novelist Jonathan Lethem published a 208-page deconstruction of *They Live* (1988), which remains filmmaker John Carpenter's cult-favoritest work today.

"DON'T PANIC"

—DOUGLAS ADAMS, *THE HITCHHIKER'S GUIDE TO THE GALAXY*

WHEN *DUNE* AUTHOR Frank Herbert referred to fear as a mind killer, he composed an entire litany to emphasize that point. On the other hand, Douglas Adams was able to convey the same sentiment with two simple words in all caps. While *The Hitchhiker's Guide* had the above legend emblazoned on its cover to avoid discouraging those who might fear the titular device was too complicated, no less an authority than Arthur C. Clarke called it the best possible advice for humankind. It's not about whether life will throw a you curveball, because if you've spent any time at all as part of the human experience, you know the odds are already pretty well stacked in favor of that happening. But the true test is how you react once the inevitable occurs. Don't be overwhelmed. Don't be discouraged. Don't. Panic. In fact, once you step back and think things through, you may just find, as Adams said elsewhere in the guide, that the whole thing is "mostly harmless."

The phrase "Don't panic" was subsequently used by a young Neil Gaiman as the title of his nonfiction book—most recently rereleased in 2009—about Douglas Adams and *The Hitchhiker's Guide*.

"AT LEAST I HAVE CHICKEN."

—LEEROY JENKINS, *WORLD OF WARCRAFT*

SOCIAL ISOLATION is an unavoidable part of the geek maturation process. It's tough being different during childhood and adolescence, given the immense social pressure to conform imposed by family, society, and schoolmates. This is why, when geeks finally find one another and form their own groups, nothing short of nuclear assault will sever those hard-won social bonds. Take, for instance, the Leeroy Jenkins incident: a now-infamous *World of Warcraft* video from 2005, documenting a game in which a whole players' guild was decimated thanks to the foolishly enthusiastic recklessness of one member who went wildly charging into battle, oblivious to the group's well-thought-out plan. Everyone from Conan O'Brien to the U.S. armed forces has cited this video as an example of crass stupidity and poor communications (on Leeroy's part) as well as taking things too seriously (that would be his fellow gamers, who grew very upset with him). But there's a more important message in the way Leeroy's guild reacted when he ignored their elaborate plan and ran straight into a deadly lions' den: *They all followed him.* They tried to save him, even though it meant that all their characters died in the process. Because, see, that's how geek friends roll.

The literal meaning of Leeroy's final comeback to his friends, "At least I have chicken," is harder to explain. Supposedly, the reason Leeroy's player Ben Schulz didn't understand the plan is because, while it was being made, he'd gone to the kitchen to get some dinner. Whether this is true is open for debate.

"THERE ARE FOUR LIGHTS!"

—JEAN-LUC PICARD, *STAR TREK: THE NEXT GENERATION*

TORTURE DOESN'T WORK . . . because torture does work. When you mindfuck people, you can't be certain how their minds will respond. Sometimes they'll give you the truth you're looking for. Sometimes they'll be determined not to, and your efforts to force it out of them risk turning untruths into their new reality. Can you tell the difference? Maybe. Or maybe not. Torture isn't just when a Cardassian officer ties up Captain Picard in the dark and uses pain to seek military intelligence. Torture is when a school bully smacks a kid in the face every single day for three years. It's when a spouse abuses the intimacy of a marriage to turn a would-be partner into a frightened slave. It's not only a cruel game, it's a dangerous one—because if the powerless ones suddenly find themselves unexpectedly holding a weapon, heaven only knows where they may end up pointing it.

The 1992 episode "Chain of Command," whence this quote comes, was cowritten by Ronald D. Moore, who later explored torture in outer space at much greater lengths in *Battlestar Galactica.*

"I CAN KILL YOU WITH MY BRAIN."

—RIVER TAM, *FIREFLY*

GEEKDOM IS A CELEBRATION of the mind. There are lots of athletic or physically attractive geeks out there, but in the end geek identity is centered on the intellect and the willingness to be different. Unfortunately, these qualities are not much celebrated in wider society. So how cool is it that in so much of geek literature—science fiction and fantasy, in other words—there are people who can kick ass with brain- and willpower? The enduring popularity of the psychic or psionic in the geek zeitgeist is ultimately about the power of the mind and its relative worth in society. The heroes and heroines of these tales often fear their power or struggle to control it—but once they've mastered it, no force in the 'verse can stop them.

Firefly (2002) may not have lasted more than fourteen episodes, but a decade later its star, Nathan Fillion, could still be found dropping in-jokes on his new TV show *Castle*.

"YOU HAVE BEEN WEIGHED, YOU HAVE BEEN MEASURED, AND YOU HAVE BEEN FOUND WANTING."

—COUNT ADHEMAR, *A KNIGHT'S TALE*

WHAT A DELICIOUSLY *utter* prick Count Adhemar was, getting off on squashing the hopes and dreams of earnest young would-be knight Sir Ulrich von Lichtenstein, aka William Thatcher. Do you know a guy like this? A guy who's totally impressed with himself for having the great genius and talent to have gotten himself born the favored son of a wealthy family of society's ruling class? Who takes it for granted that he deserves to be handsome, deserves to win trophies, deserves to have the ladies fawn all over him? You'd kinda like to knock him off a horse, wouldn't you, with a big stick and a satisfying crashing sound? Well, we're gonna be honest: You probably won't get the chance to do that. But you can imagine it. And you can take quietly sadistic comfort in the fact that, eventually, whether or not you're there to see it, he's going to zig when he should have zagged, and the look on his face just before it abruptly smacks into the ground will be all you might have hoped.

A Knight's Tale (2001) included the character of a wayward young Geoffrey Chaucer, who hadn't yet written *The Canterbury Tales*. Anyone who enjoyed the fictionalized Chaucer performed by Paul Bettany would do well to explore the separate but equally entertaining online world of *Geoffrey Chaucer Hath a Blog*.

"TWO AND TWO MAKE FIVE."

—GEORGE ORWELL, *1984*

MATHEMATICAL EQUATIONS should be frightening only to elementary school children, but there is something chilling about the above equation: a reminder that no matter how strong we think we are, the mind is weak. We all think we're smart, perceptive, and, beyond all else, rational—geeks especially think highly of the machine that is their mind, and often for good reason—but fear, oppression, and hopelessness are weapons that can savage any mind. Goebbels and the Nazi propagandists whipped a country into a frenzy of genocidal hatred not because the German people were weak minded—to the contrary, the Germans have often been intellectual pioneers—but because a person's mind is softer than flesh. Take advantage of fear (rational or otherwise), of prejudice, of want and desire, and a mind can be broken easier than a bone. Otherwise good people can be brainwashed to look away while millions are sent to their deaths, to ignore the stench of decay and pretend that, yes, two plus two does indeed make five.

George Orwell's *1984* is one of a handful of dark-geek science-fiction novels that has long enjoyed the official sanction of the academic literary canon.

"I'VE GOT A BAD FEELING ABOUT THIS."

—HAN SOLO, *STAR WARS*

"I HAVE A BAD FEELING ABOUT THIS."

—PRINCESS LEIA, *THE EMPIRE STRIKES BACK*

"I HAVE A REALLY BAD FEELING ABOUT THIS."

—HAN SOLO, *RETURN OF THE JEDI*

WHEN THE CHARACTERS in *Star Wars* have a bad feeling about something—which they frequently do, since it's the longest running and most familiar gag of the entire saga—the humor comes at the metatextual level: That statement having been uttered, the viewer knows a twist in the narrative is imminent. Life isn't much different. Sometimes you *know* something just isn't right. Whether it's fate or instinct or the subconscious mind at work, we have a way of recognizing when the walls of life's trash compactor are about to start closing in. It's that tingle in your gut that says, "If I take one more step, I'm going to lose control of the situation." That feeling, alarming though it may be, is a healthy one. Experiencing it means you're experiencing life, which means that, although by definition you can't know what unexpectedly curving path you may one day find yourself diverted into, you can rest assured there's one coming eventually. Just as "I've got a bad feeling about this" is a playful wink to the audience, the real thing is life's wink at you. Keep an eye out for it.

Other characters who've said it: Obi-Wan Kenobi, Anakin Skywalker, Luke Skywalker, C-3PO.

"HE IS THE ONE."

—MORPHEUS, *THE MATRIX*

"I KNOW KUNG FU."

—NEO, *THE MATRIX*

MOST CRITICAL ANALYSES of the *Matrix* films are quick to point out its Christian religious allegory—despite Jesus never having done much in the way of flying around or looking cool, and his method of dealing with enemies was to love them, not beat them to a bloody pulp. Neo's un-Messianic behavior may stem from the fact that "turn the other cheek" is a tough sell to geeks, many of whom have endured bullying and other forms of societal injustice. Neo—like other superheroes, into whose ranks he neatly fits—makes a more palatable savior for some because he not only rejects injustice but *attacks* it, in a wholly visceral and satisfying way. But Neo isn't very Jesus-like in another, perhaps more chilling way. The *Matrix* franchise makes much of the fact that "blue-pills" are all potential enemies, working for the system and able to be essentially possessed by Agents at any given time. Yet they are still, in essence, innocent bystanders. And although Jesus made an effort to save such people, casting out demons and calming mobs, Neo mowed them down with machine guns and flying roundhouse kicks.

Neo, then, is not Jesus. He is a savior, but only of those who ask; a redeemer, but only for those (his fellow red-pills) who are as knowledgeable and savvy as he is. His miracles are the result of his programming knowledge and mastery of the operating system that is the Matrix; he wields knowledge itself as a weapon. In this he is merely human, and deeply flawed at that. But he is, at least, a true geek avatar.

Comic-book geeks continue to squabble with movie geeks about whether the name Morpheus, out of context, should be taken as a reference to Laurence Fishburne's character in *The Matrix* or to the protagonist of Neil Gaiman's *Sandman*.

"ALL YOUR BASE ARE BELONG TO US."

— *ZERO WING* VIDEO GAME

*Z*ERO WING WAS A CLASSIC example of early video game imports, which were frequently plagued by semicomprehensible "Japlish"—an affectionate term for Japanese dialogue translated badly into English by companies too cheap or too broke to localize the game properly. Even by the rough standards of the day, however, *Zero Wing*'s translation was so awful that it achieved a kind of surreal artistic brilliance. "All your base are belong to us"—dear lord, there are tense problems, plurality problems, passive-voice problems, all in the span of seven words. But mangled or not, the quintessential sense of betrayal communicated by such *Zero Wing* phrases as "somebody set us up the bomb" was painfully clear, which may be why so many geeks used the phrase in response to any kind of double-cross or undeserved attack. There was something poetic about it all, even if unintentionally so. In 2003, teenagers in Sturgis, Michigan, posted "All your base . . . " signs all over town—purportedly as an April Fool's Day protest against the war in Iraq, lending these flubbed translations an even greater social-justice significance. Not bad for an otherwise mediocre game.

Zero Wing was originally an arcade game in Japan (1989) before being ported to Sega home systems and desktop PCs several years later.

"OH, BOY."

—DR. SAM BECKETT, *QUANTUM LEAP*

ONE OF THE MOST IMPORTANT things in life is maintaining the proper perspective—realizing that no matter how important or Earth-shattering our problems may seem at any given minute, 'someone else is dealing with something that, to them, is just as profound and/or just as devastating. This is something Sam Beckett became intimately familiar with, because if anything will force you to metaphorically look at the world through another person's eyes, it's literally looking at the world through another person's eyes. Sam spent five seasons exiled helplessly from his own existence, quantum-leaping into the lives (and bodies) of various unfortunates scattered across the timestream. And it tells you something that, after discovering each time that his latest leap wouldn't be the one to finally bring him home, Sam did not succumb to desperation or despondency. He just allowed himself a momentary respite, a succinct "Oh, boy." Then he got down to the business of setting right what once went wrong.

Here's some really obscure geek trivia: Allan Sherman, the 1960s song-parodist precursor to Weird Al Yankovic who wrote "Hello Muddah, Hello Faddah," also recorded a little ditty titled "Oh, Boy." Sadly, Sam Beckett never met him onscreen.

"NOBODY EXPECTS THE SPANISH INQUISITION!"

—*MONTY PYTHON'S FLYING CIRCUS*

"WHAT IS THE AIR-SPEED VELOCITY OF AN UNLADEN SWALLOW?"

—*MONTY PYTHON AND THE HOLY GRAIL*

W E SEEK SOLACE IN SILLINESS. This was the simple formula the madcap sketch-comedy geniuses of Monty Python stumbled upon as they shone their uniquely British (well, five Brits and a Yank) spotlight on all manner of absurdist tableaus—whether the aforementioned Spanish Inquisitors busting anachronistically into a scene far removed in time and space from their own, or a pet-shop owner insisting that a stiff and motionless parrot is most certainly not dead, or an armless and legless Black Knight defiantly proclaiming that it's "just a flesh wound." Indeed, so influential were these funnymen in reshaping the landscape of millennial humor that the very term *Pythonesque* has garnered inclusion in dictionaries as a signifier of the loopy, punch-drunk surrealism that their routines encourage each of us to free inside ourselves. You might not think it on those days when you're up at six, stuck in bumper-to-bumper traffic, and headed to a job you despise working for a boss you detest, but sometimes the only way to empower yourself and push back against the various vicissitudes life throws at you is to take a step back, see yourself as part of an awesomely ridiculous joke that's as big as the whole damn universe, and just let yourself laugh out loud at it, whether or not anyone else thinks it makes a lick of sense. It *doesn't.* That's why it's funny.

Monty Python's Flying Circus originally aired on the BBC from late 1969 through 1974. For geek context: That's the Jon Pertwee era of *Doctor Who*.

"I SAY WE TAKE OFF AND NUKE THE SITE FROM ORBIT."

—RIPLEY, *ALIENS*

MOVIE LOGIC FRUSTRATES most geeks. It just doesn't make sense for the people in a horror film to go one by one to investigate that strange noise in the dark—that didn't work out so well for the last five people, did it? It's *stupid* for the evil overlord to capture the intrepid hero and then leave him alone in a room full of convenient tools; any overlord with a brain would just kill the guy right off. All too often, Hollywood characters choose the more dramatic path through hardship rather than the smart one. This was why the *Alien* films were such a breath of fresh air. Ripley, faced with a planetary colony full to overflowing with unstoppably murderous alien beasts, actually understood what she was up against. Never mind trying to safely capture an alien—it *wasn't going to happen*. Ripley pushed instead for the Occam's Razor method of problem-solving: simple, overwhelming, effective. Thus "take off and nuke the site from orbit" has become geek shorthand for putting a decisive end to any dangerously messy problem. Overkill? Maybe. But sometimes you just have to be sure.

In our personal version of the *Alien* universe, Newt and Ripley and the cat are all off somewhere living happily ever after. They deserve it.

"IT'S DANGEROUS TO GO ALONE!
TAKE THIS."

—CAPTION FROM *THE LEGEND OF ZELDA*, TURNED INTO A LOLCAT MEME

S MART PEOPLE ARE OFTEN self-sufficient and confident, particularly when it comes to our particular area(s) of expertise. The average geek is often the only person in the group who's capable of solving some arcane and specialized problem. Which presents a whole 'nother problem: Even though geeky confidence and competence can sometimes lead to obnoxious and undeserved arrogance, the plain fact of the matter is that, frequently, when it comes to a particular topic, the geek really is the most knowledgeable person in the room. That doesn't stop other people from trying to help, though—often with contributions that seem absurd or useless. The foolish geek rolls his or her eyes at these offers of help, but the wise geek takes them as they're meant: a sincere desire to share in the geeky joy of problem-solving. And hey, you never know—that doofus might just have a point.

Please feel free to consider this book as a "this" that just might possibly be helpful.

"NOW WE KNOW. AND KNOWING IS HALF THE BATTLE!"

—G.I. JOE (CARTOON)

G.I. JOE, like many cartoons of the 1980s, taught us the meaning of irony. Every week, after watching a privately funded mercenary squad fire thousands of lasers, missiles, and BFGs at its enemies, we then endured a brief lecture on morality, including the need to resolve problems without violence. But we saw no real contradiction in this, since compartmentalization is a necessary and welcome part of the geek mindset. How else are we to keep separate our many realms—not just our fictional realms of fantasy and science fiction and role-playing games, but our real-world realms of entertainment, work, and social life? So ingrained is our ability to suspend disbelief at will, and to separate fantasy from reality, that we are often stunned when non-geeks *don't* do this, or don't believe us when we say we can. Could this be why we embrace the fantastic, while non-geeks frequently fear or disdain it?

One of the great triumphs in the field of Internet snark is the viral-hit G.I. Joe–themed pie chart in which we are informed that "The Battle" is made up of 50 percent knowing, 25 percent red lasers, and 25 percent blue lasers.

"FLY CASUAL!"

—HAN SOLO, *RETURN OF THE JEDI*

O R: "NEVER LET 'EM SEE YOU SWEAT." Or: "There is nothing to fear but fear itself." Attempting to sneak past an imperial blockade in which Darth Vader's cruiser is close enough to scratch the paint, smuggler-turned-rebel-general Han Solo uses humor and a little bit of swagger to assure his crew that all is well, even as most of us would quiver and crumble under similarly dire circumstances. That is why we love Han. Not because he doesn't feel the same panic we all do, but because he doesn't allow it to cripple him; instead he finds a way to power through it. Granted, the line between swagger and stupidity can be thin, and only the passage of time will determine which side we end up on. Regardless of the aphorism you wrap it in, the sentiment expressed by Solo—casual confidence in the face of insurmountable odds—is not only what we hope to see in our leaders, it's what we hope to find inside ourselves.

There are geeks who opine that *Return of the Jedi* (1983) was where the *Star Wars* saga began to stink. There are a handful of still geekier geeks itching to one-up them and claim *Empire* is where it went wrong. *Those* geeks? Even we want to give them wedgies.

"AS AN ONLINE DISCUSSION
GROWS LONGER,
THE PROBABILITY OF
A COMPARISON INVOLVING
NAZIS OR HITLER
APPROACHES 1."

—MIKE GODWIN, GODWIN'S LAW

GEEKS LOVE TO FIGHT, and those fights are often epic in their awesomeness. The advent of the Internet merely updated a longstanding geek tradition of launching interpersonal battles over minutiae—which, prior to the Internet, expressed itself in the form of months-long arguments in the "Letters to the Editor" columns of comic books, dueling Cthulhu Mythos tales in fanzines, and so on. But the Internet also made it clear that geek arguments follow a predictable pattern—and any  dispute that goes on long enough will always, inevitably, reach the "scorched earth" stage, past which any discussion becomes irrelevant. (Oh, so preferring Batman's black-armored movie costume to his classic grey tights is the opinion of, not just *another guy*, but a *jackbooted fascist*? Really, boywonder953? Really?) This has become such a truism that weary blog commenters, smelling a nasty fight in the making, will often preemptively mention Nazis just to cut things short. And it's alarming to see that the non-geek portions of the media have taken the same path; heck, the Jon Stewart/Stephen Colbert rally of 2010 was mostly an attempt to ask, "Can we please stop calling each other Hitler?" It would seem the answer is no.

At least some geeks are fighting to take back the Hitler epithet in the name of good-spirited silliness. Thousands of YouTube videos have mashed up a scene in the Hitler bio-film *Downfall* with topics ranging from Xbox to *Twilight*.

"I LOVE IT WHEN A PLAN COMES TOGETHER!"

—JOHN "HANNIBAL" SMITH, *THE A-TEAM*

HAN SOLO MAY HAVE SHOWN us the seat-of-your-pants thrill of improvising, but Hannibal Smith taught us there's something to be said for taking the long view. And one thing you can't accuse the jocular leader of the A-Team of is not taking the long view, with his daisy-chain schemas of elaborate disguises, car crashes, and lots of pyrotechnics making it all the sweeter when he deployed his trademark catchphrase as the payoff to a job well done. As Smith and his *Team*-mates showed week in and week out between 1983 and 1987 (and once in 2010), sometimes planning isn't about anticipating every exigency down to the last detail; it's about knowing how to react when the unexpected occurs. He may never have led an army across the Alps atop elephants, like the Carthiginian general from whom he took his name, Hannibal nonetheless exemplified the same lesson: The bigger the risk, the greater the need for planning—and the bigger the thrill when it falls into place.

Geek thrills that follow much the same principle: dominos, Rube Goldberg machines, and Odyssey of the Mind tournaments.

"DON'T CROSS THE STREAMS. IT WOULD BE BAD."

—EGON SPENGLER, *GHOSTBUSTERS*

EGON'S WARNING TO his fellow Ghostbusters was perhaps the most casually deadpan mention of possibly accidentally blowing oneself to bits ever committed to voice. It's typical, though. In the eyes of mainstream society, most geeks tend to get excited by all the "wrong" things. From raging battles over which is the best X-Man to the abject joy that ripples through nerddom whenever a new Hubble image is released, there's no doubt that geeks are passionate people. Yet, all this passion for offbeat, unique things sometimes leaves little room in our cerebral cortex for getting excited about relatively ordinary things . . . like, say, the possibility of a violent horrific death. Death, after all, happens to everyone; there's nothing especially unique about it. But *a Goldilocks-zone exoplanet*? Now that's worth an exclamation point or two. Of course, this means that whenever a geek laconically suggests that taking a particular course of action "would be bad," those passionate about their own continued well-being should probably pay really, really close attention.

Hey, what's a Goldilocks-zone exoplanet, anyway? We're gonna let you look that one up. Consider it an exercise in geekiness.

**"JOIN THE ARMY,
MEET INTERESTING PEOPLE,
AND KILL THEM."**
—STEVEN WRIGHT

**"ITS FIVE-YEAR MISSION:
TO EXPLORE STRANGE
NEW WORLDS."**
—OPENING NARRATION, *STAR TREK*

**"I WILL GOUGE OUT
YOUR EYES AND
SKULLF— YOU!"**
—GUNNERY SERGEANT HARTMAN, *FULL METAL JACKET*

THE MILITARY REPRESENTS a jumble of mixed feelings for young geeks, and Steven Wright's classic one-line gag pretty much sums it up. Growing up on a diet of epic adventure stories tends to cultivate a sense of romanticism, which means we get excited at the prospect of sharing a quest with a band of comrades, of taking part in a grand struggle that's greater than ourselves. Also, we love tech—and who has better gadgets than the military. On the other hand, our natural inclination to always question authority, to push back against dogma, means that we chafe against any sort of hierarchical command structure that might require us to take direction from anyone whose view of the universe is smaller and meaner than our own. It's no coincidence that Gene Roddenberry changed the broad face of science fiction by creating a tale that managed to have it both ways: Starfleet is a military-structured organization whose first mission is peaceful exploration; the *Enterprise* carries a crew who are willing to buck the rules whenever they think it's necessary, and, miraculously, they almost always turn out to be right. There's no screaming drill sergeant threatening to rip out a trainee's eyes in *Star Trek*, and there's rarely an Abu Ghraib, either. (That's why the rougher, rawer *Battlestar Galactica*, not *Trek*, was the science-fiction success story of the 2000s.) Could there ever be a real Starfleet—a force using military organization to effectively promote individual accomplishment throughout its sphere of action? Countless disillusioned Peace Corps vets suggest no—and yet our geeky hearts still want to say yes.

Colonel Tigh, the drill-sergeant archetype in *Galactica*, was the one who got his eye gouged out. We're pretty sure that's irony.

"TO LEARN WHICH QUESTIONS ARE UNANSWERABLE, AND NOT ANSWER THEM: THIS SKILL IS MOST NEEDFUL IN TIMES OF STRESS AND DARKNESS."

—URSULA LE GUIN, *THE LEFT HAND OF DARKNESS*

SOMETIMES, SCI-FI CHARACTERS offering advice veer into the realm of the overcooked. But sometimes a piece of wisdom hits you right between the eyes. Geeks in particular have a tendency to overthink—to insist on making sense of everything from every angle so we might come at an answer from a place of omnipotence. As nice a situation as that might be, reality generally precludes it; we live in a quick-and-dirty world that functions largely on snap decision and compromise. That can often take some adjustment for geeks, who prefer their world-building logical and their decisions foolproof. And it's disheartening to realize that the world is also far more stress and darkness than sweetness and light. The good news is that if anyone can separate the components of a situation and solve only for the bug-free variables, it's geeks. The trick is to recognize the unsolvable when it appears; there, you're on your own.

A counterpart to Le Guin's point has been expressed in the realm of pure mathematics: Gödel's Incompleteness Theorem (1931) says that any mathematical system will include facts about the natural numbers that are true, yet cannot be proved.

"THIS IS MY BOOMSTICK."

—ASH, ARMY OF DARKNESS

WE LOVED ASH in *Evil Dead* and *Evil Dead 2*, but it was in *Army of Darkness*, when he played a modern-day Yankee in King—er, Lord—Arthur's court, that he really shone. And we loved it, because Ash was a geek *and* a badass. He knew more than everyone around him. He was unversed in the social graces of the era, but that was okay; he made his own rules. We also loved the subtle critique of geekiness that the film displayed. Ash's cockiness made him his own worst enemy, and his love life might have turned out a lot better if he hadn't been such an ass. But he didn't care about those things, either. In the end, it was his confidence, deserved or not, that made him powerful and admirable. Even if some of us never did forgive him for screwing up *klaatu barada nikto*. He lost some geek points for that one.

Geek Hall of Fame alert: Bruce Campbell's portrayal of Ash kicked off a career that spanned such cult classics as *Bubba Ho-tep*, *Escape from L.A.*, *Xena: Warrior Princess*, and *The Adventures of Brisco County Jr.*

"THE FIRST RULE OF FIGHT CLUB IS: YOU DO NOT TALK ABOUT FIGHT CLUB."

—TYLER DURDEN, *FIGHT CLUB*

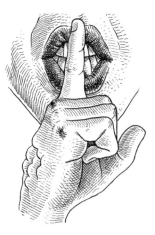

THERE'S SOMETHING to be said for exclusivity. After all, haven't you ever had a favorite band that you lived and breathed until it committed the cardinal sin of becoming too popular? Haven't you had a favorite movie you began to hate once everyone else started quoting it? Didn't Facebook lose some of its luster when you got that friend request from your great-aunt Polly? The "fight club" at the center of Chuck Palahniuk's book and David Fincher's film isn't so much a social movement as it is that hardcore indie band you just don't want to see sell out. But that's the inherent problem with anything that impacts society enough to bring about lasting change: Its success carries within it the seeds of its eventual dissolution. If history teaches us anything, it's that the rebels of today are inevitably the establishmentarians of tomorrow—whether Fidel Castro, Kurt Cobain, or Mark Zuckerberg. And so, can you really blame Tyler Durden for wanting to keep a lid on his new favorite thing for just a little while longer?

The novel *Fight Club* (1996) established Chuck Palahniuk as a major author of disturbing fiction. His short story "Guts," about unfortunate masturbation accidents, established him as an author who could cause people to faint while listening to him read out loud.

"TO CRUSH YOUR ENEMIES, SEE THEM DRIVEN BEFORE YOU, AND TO HEAR THE LAMENTATION OF THEIR WOMEN."

—CONAN, *CONAN THE BARBARIAN*

THE HEARTLESSNESS OF THE CONQUEROR is something most people are incapable of understanding. We are empathetic beings; the roots of our greatest civilizations, and thus our greatest accomplishments, lie in our inherently social nature. Even we geeks—solitary creatures of the modern world—feel the same pull. The great conquerors did not. For Alexander of Macedon, life was the campaign. For Genghis Khan, a day dawning without plumes of smoke rising from the cities behind him was not a day worth living. Napoleon Bonaparte's conquests were not an expansion of the French Revolution and the 'emperor's ideals, but a result of his irrepressible need to run roughshod over others. These were great men in their own way, men whose deeds help continue history's inexorable march toward the modern world. But they were also troubled in a way most of us cannot grasp. Considering the broken families and endless gravestones left in their wake, maybe we ought to be glad that such greatness is rare.

Conan's most famous quote from *Conan the Barbarian* (1982) comes not from the classic stories by author Robert E. Howard but is adapted from an anecdote related in the 1927 Genghis Khan biography, *Emperor of All Men.*

"SOME DAYS, YOU JUST CAN'T GET RID OF A BOMB."

—BATMAN, *BATMAN* (1966)

TRUER WORDS have never been spoken, you know? Of course, you'd never expect Batman to have a problem disposing of a bomb—the man has a handmade tool belt that navigates a submarine, for crying out loud—but this is the Adam West version we're talking about. Of all the Batman incarnations, this deliberately cartoonish take on the savior of Gotham ruined Batman's street cred with the other superheroes for decades afterward. It's comforting in its own way to think that, even if we can't have sound-effect bubbles when we head out for capers, we can at least relate to Batman every time we have an explosive situation that can't be easily dismissed. (Figuratively . . . we hope.) It's understandable that sometimes a situation is more than you can clean up. The world is a tricky place, and, superhero or not, sometimes you just can't make a problem go away.

Legendary ham Adam West and legendary ham William Shatner appeared together in an early-1960s pilot for the would-be television adventures of Alexander the Great. Alas, it didn't happen, and we had to settle for Kirk and Batman.

"REPENT! THE END IS EXTREMELY F—KING NIGH!"

—28 DAYS LATER

THE AWKWARD THING about living in a postmodern world is the general expectation that everyone has a quip ready to go when the monsters attack. (If you don't have one ready, think of one now. We'll wait; this is important.) The darker side of general-monster-preparedness is the accompanying general expectation that we'll all be able to handle it with the aplomb of a balding franchise headliner, when really, if hideous hordes ever came at us snarling and clawing, it would be exactly as horrific as it sounds. In the Internet age, a lot of cultural cool-points are derived from seeming jaded enough to joke about genuinely terrible things; as we've noted, many an Internet meme has sprung up around natural and humanitarian disasters. While humor is a well-known coping strategy, there's also nothing wrong with getting upset for the right reasons—so go ahead and call bullshit when people dismiss problems that you know matter. And if you get shit for it, you have a quip ready to go! (Emergency preparedness: Geeks have it.)

The zombie film *28 Days Later* (2002) gains extra geek points on top of its fundamental awesomeness for featuring Christopher Eccleston, who three years later would star in the triumphantly relaunched *Doctor Who*.

"THERE'S ONLY ONE RULE THAT I KNOW OF, BABIES—GOD DAMN IT, YOU'VE GOT TO BE KIND."

—KURT VONNEGUT

MAN SHOWS INHUMANITY TO MAN. It's axiomatic of our existence. It's the story of our past, it's the story of our present, and it will very likely be the story of our future. Indeed, it's a lesson that's reinforced every day, whether we're watching the evening news or the latest entry in the *Saw* series. However, our history is also littered with awe-inspiring examples of men and women showing incredible compassion in the face of unspeakable evil and insurmountable odds. Every story of tragedy has a story of heroism to go with it. For every Holocaust, there's a Schindler. Vonnegut's words, spoken so simply, are nonetheless laced with considerable profundity. The imperative to be kind to one another may seem obvious, but part of being human means that both the right thing and the wrong thing are forever at arm's reach. It doesn't hurt to be reminded every now and then which one we should choose.

Vonnegut's novel *God Bless You, Mr. Rosewater* (1965) is less overtly geeky than the likes of *Slaughterhouse-Five*, *Breakfast of Champions*, and *The Sirens of Titan*, but aside from being just as great, it does tie into the rest with several cameo appearances.

"SO SAY WE ALL."

—BILL ADAMA, *BATTLESTAR GALACTICA*

W E HOLD THESE TRUTHS TO BE SELF-EVIDENT, that all men are created equal." These words, from the American Declaration of Independence, represent an admirable ideal that America took rather a long time to live up to. Fortunately for most of us, these words eventually came to represent more than landowning white men. Bill Adama was *Battlestar Galactica*'s Thomas Jefferson, and *BSG* was, at its heart, the story of a nation's formation. Like Jefferson, Adama was a man of great contradiction: a supposed visionary who lied about the vision (the mythical existence of Earth); an authoritarian who turned out to be more democratic in principle than the democratically elected president he served; a confessed bigot who allied with, and even came to love, the objects of his hatred. The resolution of the story ultimately came down to the question of whether disparate groups—military and civilian, human and Cylon, even humanoid Cylon and robotic Centurion—could learn first to recognize one another as people, then to live together. Eventually, they did. Thus Adama's words, which first applied only to members of the military under his own command, came to embrace all of humankind, and humanity's children as well.

Bill Adama was actor Edward James Olmos's second chance to explore dangerous, artificially created humanoids; the first was *Blade Runner* (1982).

"MISTER MCGEE, DON'T MAKE ME ANGRY. YOU WOULDN'T LIKE ME WHEN I'M ANGRY."

—DAVID BRUCE BANNER, *THE INCREDIBLE HULK*

"PARDON ME FOR BREATHING, WHICH I NEVER DO ANYWAY SO I DON'T KNOW WHY I BOTHER TO SAY IT, OH GOD I'M SO DEPRESSED."

—MARVIN, *THE HITCHHIKER'S GUIDE TO THE GALAXY*

GEEKS notoriously have trouble expressing emotion. That's why Spock became our great iconic hero: he, too, dealt with the confusing struggle of his feelings by burying them beneath a near-fanatic devotion to intellectual calculations and philosophical ponderings. And the fact that he came from a whole race of people like that gave us hope that maybe we weren't as pathetic and alone in our fear of emotional vulnerability as we thought we were. Doctor Banner's famous line from the opening credits of *The Incredible Hulk* perfectly encapsulates this inner turmoil, saying what all repressed geeks wants to say whenever people try to get under their skin: *I have made staying in control of myself a firm rule of life, and I fear that out-of-control me will be something terrible to behold, so why don't you just not make me go there.* The flip side of this phenomenon is the cynical geek who, rather than burying all emotion beneath reason, buries any explicit acknowledgment of idealism or romance beneath a protective shield of pessimism: because this geek "knows everything already," you see, there's nothing to get excited about. That, in a nutshell is Marvin, the super-genius robot in Douglas Adams's *Hitchhikers Guide to the Galaxy*—he wants you to know just how depressing the whole world is, because it can't possibly present anything new or interesting to him. But it *could*, if he'd let it—just as Spock, Banner, and all the other nerds out there could figure out how to enjoy being a little bit out of control once in a while if they'd just stop envisioning their primitive impulses as a terrifying, rampaging monster.

"VIOLENCE IS THE LAST REFUGE OF THE INCOMPETENT."

—HARI SELDON, *FOUNDATION*

INTELLECTUALS BELIEVE in the power of the mind. If you have to resort to force, you've already failed. This is a noble and admirable belief, and muchly if not entirely true—but there's something more interesting at work here. We all tend to believe that our own best characteristic represents "true strength," just as we're all instinctively inclined to believe that a person who agrees with us a lot must be a very smart person indeed. Therefore, as intellectuals, we find physical force abhorrent in the extreme, in part because it just plain is, but also in part because our self-esteem *depends* on believing that mental power is more important. At the same time, it's worth noting that, in *Foundation*, überbrainiac author Isaac Asimov deliberately crafted a story where the careful application of nonviolent smarts was able to triumph over every single violent threat that his protagonist nation faced—which rather flies in the face of all human history. Sometimes, violent people make targets of the most peace-loving among us, and the choice to fight for survival doesn't necessarily mean we're incompetent; Asimov, a WWII–era Jew, never argued in real life that military force shouldn't be employed to stop the Nazis. The key to fully embracing this quote lies in the particular diction: not *tool*, but *refuge*. Violence may be sadly necessary at times, but anyone who finds solace in its application is a poor human, indeed.

"TRY NOT. DO. OR DO NOT. THERE IS NO TRY."

—YODA, *THE EMPIRE STRIKES BACK*

YODA OFFERED LUKE SKYWALKER THIS WISDOM in reference to extricating a crashed X-Wing Fighter from the swamp on Dagobah, but he might as well have been talking to Thomas Edison as the first inklings of incandescent light germinated in his mind. He might as well have been talking to Michael Jordan as he laced up before his first college game. He might as well have been talking to you before going in for that big promotion. Far too often, our fear of running headlong into our own limitations contents us with merely trying to accomplish our goals. That way the bar is adjusted downward to mean that, hey, even if we didn't succeed, we didn't really fail either. And though there are times, sure, when the effort we invest in a task can be its own reward, let's be honest with ourselves: there are other times when effort can be measured only against its completion. So don't look for reasons why a thing can't be done. Just go ahead and make it happen.

Nike is not as wise as Yoda but does make very effective commercials.

"RAYMOND SHAW IS THE KINDEST, BRAVEST, WARMEST, MOST WONDERFUL HUMAN BEING I'VE EVER KNOWN IN MY LIFE."

—BENNETT MARCO, *THE MANCHURIAN CANDIDATE*

"YOU TAKE THE BLUE PILL, AND THE STORY ENDS; YOU WAKE IN YOUR BED AND YOU BELIEVE WHATEVER YOU WANT TO BELIEVE. YOU TAKE THE RED PILL, AND YOU STAY IN WONDERLAND AND I SHOW YOU HOW DEEP THE RABBIT HOLE GOES."

—MORPHEUS, *THE MATRIX*

W'RE BEING BRAINWASHED CONSTANTLY. Not necessarily by communists (like in 1962's *The Manchurian Candidate*) or a transnational corporation (like in the 2004 remake), but by talking points. After all, what is Ben Marco's rote description of his wartime compatriot, implanted in his mind by a sinister Sino-Russian cabal and repeated ad nauseam, but an expression of the talking points that saturate the mediasphere daily. They ensure that debate has already been framed and decided for us long in advance of our forming an actual opinion. They let us know what to think without having to do the hard work of getting there on our own. Whether we're talking about Raymond Shaw or WMD or death panels, the inherent danger of talking points is that they become so ingrained through sheer force of repetition that we're rendered incapable of seeing the reality that may be lurking just underneath. Luckily, Bennett Marco broke through his conditioning in time to give his story a semblance of a happy ending. So did Neo, who needed the symbolism of Morpheus's red pill more than he needed the pill itself. As Confucius said, the journey of a thousand miles begins with a single step. More precisely, it begins by choosing to *take* that step—even when the consequences of that choice are as yet unknown.

"I'M THE BEST THERE IS AT WHAT I DO. BUT WHAT I DO ISN'T VERY NICE."

—WOLVERINE

WRITER CHRIS CLAREMONT committed these two sentences to the page in 1982, and in doing so cemented Wolverine's place as a geek icon long before Hugh Jackman turned him into a movie idol. Although this epigraph refers to the character's lethal skill with his knuckle-knives, it could just as easily be applied to Han Solo shooting Greedo (first!), Dirty Harry roughing up Scorpio, or John Bender mouthing off to Principal Vernon. It's why we love our antiheroes: They do what we wish we could do and say what we wish we could say. In fiction, if not in life, antiheroes offer a release for the frustration we feel from the bonds of polite society, and we tacitly accept that though they may not conform to our notions of civil justice or (in the case of Bender) polite discourse, their personal codes are no less "pure." What Wolverine does is indeed not very nice—and yet there's an important addendum implicit in the above: "But it needs to be done."

Exercise in geekery: How many multisyllabic rhymes for "Wolverine" can you find? Extra credit for a complete sonnet.

"THERE CAN BE ONLY ONE."

— HIGHLANDER

IN THE DAYS WHEN VIDEO GAMES weren't much more than a bunch of squares shooting at other squares, *Highlander* vicariously offered us the ultimate concept in live-action roleplaying. The movie and TV series characters—most of them too shallow to be anything but archetypes or caricatures—satisfied a visceral urge in all of us, an unfulfilled yearning for the romanticized rugged individualism of earlier days. Thus these rampantly macho, stubbornly primitive warriors never sought to band together or forge their own society, nor did they impact society in any of the thousand ways that the presence of a separate subspecies of humanity *should have* affected the world, realistically speaking. No, they stuck to swords even into the age of Glocks and persisted in honoring their frankly nonsensical rules—e.g., no killing on holy ground—simply because to do otherwise would break character. In the end, it didn't have to make sense and wouldn't have been half as much fun if it had. Who *doesn't* secretly yearn to be able to swing a real sword, whether during a combat reenactment at the Society for Creative Anachronism or just during a bad day at work?

A friend of a friend of ours reportedly liked to utter another *Highlander* quote midcoitus: "What you feel is the quickening." This is geekery at its creepiest. Don't do it.

"TAKE YOUR STINKING PAWS OFF ME, YOU DAMN DIRTY APE."

—TAYLOR, *PLANET OF THE APES*

IMAGINE FOR A MOMENT that you're Colonel George Taylor. You've woken from the two-thousand-year nap of a one-way space trip—only to find that, of all the planets in the universe where you could possibly have landed, you *happen* to be on the one where talking, intelligent apes like to hunt human beings like you for sport. But it doesn't stop there. In rapid succession you're shot in the throat, caged, beaten, and burned. You're forced to mate in front of an audience like an animal and threatened with emasculation. You see your fellow astronaut stuffed and mounted in a museum; you're whipped, dragged by horses, and pelted with fruit. Now, in the final indignity, you're captured in a net and are being jeered and clawed at by a gathered crowd of simians. Let's face it. It's been a *bad* couple of weeks. After all that, what would *you* say? Yep. Standing up for yourself feels good, doesn't it?

"A STRANGE GAME. THE ONLY WINNING MOVE IS NOT TO PLAY."

—JOSHUA, *WAR GAMES*

THERE IS A WORD, a concept, in Zen Buddhism that doesn't quite translate perfectly into the English language: *Mu*. Mu is the response given by a Zen monk to a question that cannot be meaningfully answered. It suggests that the question's premises are not real, that there is a state of emptiness that lies beyond yes and no, that the asker should unask the question—indeed, that anyone who would ask such a question in the first place might do well to question his entire perspective on life. Though the word was never uttered in 1984's seminal teen-computer-hacker-political-thriller *War Games*, the idea lies at the heart of the conflict that fuels the movie: a new Pentagon supercomputer that controls the nation's nuclear launch codes is caught up in a relentless war-game simulation trying to answer the question, "How can the United States win a nuclear war?" *We* all know it's a flawed question—the whole point of the Cold War arms-race theory of "mutual assured destruction" was that, in a world of opposing superpowers, the sheer volume of weaponry is meant to deter the use of any nukes at all. But back in 1984, when computer networks were new and exotic, it seemed entirely reasonable to worry that an artificial intelligence might start firing missiles based on the inhuman outcome of an algorithm. Of course, the computer finally found its Zen. What about you—can *you* tell when it's time to remove yourself from a defective game board?

The first several years of Matthew Broderick's career were all about nuclear paranoia: first *War Games*, then *Project X* (1987), wherein laboratory chimps suffered inhumane radiation testing.

V.
BILLIONS
AND BILLIONS

(WISDOM ABOUT THE UNIVERSE)

"ALL THESE WORLDS ARE YOURS, EXCEPT EUROPA. ATTEMPT NO LANDING THERE."

—ARTHUR C. CLARKE, *2010: ODYSSEY TWO*

"A STARSHIP CAPTAIN'S MOST SOLEMN OATH IS THAT HE WILL GIVE HIS LIFE, EVEN HIS ENTIRE CREW, RATHER THAN VIOLATE THE PRIME DIRECTIVE."

—JAMES T. KIRK, *STAR TREK*, "THE OMEGA GLORY"

THE EARTH WON'T ALWAYS BE the only place where humankind rests its collective head. Assuming we don't destroy ourselves first, we'll one day find that our grasp extends upward and outward, to places about which only the geek has daydreamed. Considering how well we've managed this blue orb in our 5,000 years or so of recorded history, Arthur C. Clarke's warning (delivered through the entities that control his mysterious monoliths) about not treading on places that may contain life appears well founded. See, Europa is a special place. No other body in our solar system has a better chance of containing life than that ice-covered moon of Jupiter. Through wit, intelligence, and innovation we've earned the right to tread on other celestial bodies . . . but have we earned the right to interfere with life not of this Earth? With life only just beginning its own journey down the evolutionary path? Given history, it's hard to answer in the affirmative. Gene Roddenberry took this same concept and extended

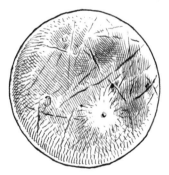

it far beyond Europa to cover the entire galaxy; the Prime Directive of *Star Trek* is that Starfleet officers must not interfere with the natural development of less technologically advanced alien species. And though Captain Kirk did somersaults around that directive as often as he followed it, his success at doing so seems to be the exception that proves the rule.

Europa is the sixth moon of Jupiter. Galileo discovered it (see next page). It has an oxygen atmosphere. And NASA and the European Space Agency hope to send a joint unmanned mission there circa 2020 to get a closer look.

"THE BOOK OF NATURE IS WRITTEN IN THE LANGUAGE OF MATHEMATICS."

—GALILEO, *THE ASSAYER*

NEVER MIND THAT THERE ARE geometric shapes in mineral crystals, fractals in vegetables, chaotic equations in weather patterns. We get all that. Galileo was onto something even deeper: the idea that nature itself could be read and encapsulated as a book or any other comprehensible source of information, rather than simply elided as beyond human understanding. This, of course, is what got him into trouble with the Catholic Church, which positioned itself as the defending champion in the age-old contest of the spirit versus reason—or, more precisely, politics versus facts. There is that indefinable something in the geek nature that rejects such distinctions as a false dichotomy, insisting that reason informs the spirit and politics should be rooted in facts. Sadly, society just isn't that rational, as Galileo discovered after his prosecution and lifelong house arrest by the Inquisition. Yet it was Galileo's geekish insistence that he was right, and his willingness to die to prove his rightness—and, mind you, the fact that he *was* right, which matters—that helped make the world a safer place for proper geekery. For this, as much as for his scientific accomplishments, he should be celebrated.

Galileo's scientific manifesto *The Assayer* (1623) was written primarily as a slam against Jesuit astronomer Orazio Grassi. In doing so, Galileo pissed off a number of Jesuit scholars who might otherwise have stood with him during his Church troubles. Trolling: risky since 1623.

"TO A NEW WORLD OF GODS AND MONSTERS!"

—DR. PRETORIUS, *BRIDE OF FRANKENSTEIN*

I N TOASTING HIS IMPENDING CREATION of a mate for Dr. Henry Frankenstein's misbegotten monster, Septimus Pretorius betrays a barely concealed glee at his impending traversal of the boundaries between the laws of man and the laws of god. In that glee, he anticipated the new world that would arrive just a few years hence, birthed in the crucible of science, where man's ability to harness the power of the atom would elevate him to godhood, and the subsequent unleashing of that power would debase him to monsterhood. The simple lesson of Pretorius, and Frankenstein before him, is the need for man to balance his unending thirst for knowledge—the "what" and the "how" and even the "why"—with the consequences of that knowledge—the "what next." Simple enough to make the enduring appeal of Mary Shelley's immortal story (and its most famous movie sequel) easy to understand but, unfortunately for us, not so simple that we've taken that lesson to heart.

Bride of Frankenstein (1939), for all its good points, might well have faded into obscurity as an unnecessary follow-up to a self-contained classic if not for the incredible power of the pure visual. The Bride's iconic two-tone tower of a hairdo ensured that she could never be forgotten.

"THE CLAW IS OUR MASTER. THE CLAW DECIDES WHO WILL GO AND WHO WILL STAY."

—VENDING MACHINE ALIEN DOLLS, *TOY STORY*

EVERY ONCE IN A WHILE, you meet someone who just doesn't seem to know what the deal is. They sit next to you in the movie theater and guess the plot loudly and incorrectly; they laugh at the joke three lines before the punch line. Usually the culprit is a fundamental glitch in perspective. The dolls stuck in *Toy Story*'s claw-grab machine don't understand the scope of the world, because they literally have no outside perspective. And yet, even as we smile at them, the alien dolls are a source of pity; their myopia is a result of circumstances beyond their control; they're victims of their own little plushie predestination. It can be tempting to dismiss those whose views differ fundamentally from ours in ways that make us socially uncomfortable. However, it's worth remembering that everyone is a victim of circumstance in one way or another, and that when one is under the regime of the Claw, it can be hard to get a good look at the larger universe.

The Claw is not to be confused with *Inspector Gadget*'s villainous Dr. Klaw, voiced by animation legend Frank Welker, who is also Megatron, Baby Kermit, and Fred from *Scooby-Doo*.

"NOW I AM BECOME DEATH, THE DESTROYER OF WORLDS."

—J. ROBERT OPPENHEIMER, QUOTING/TRANSLATING THE *BHAGAVAD GITA*

IMAGINE, IF YOU WILL, being central to the development of a power that could snuff out tens of thousands of lives in an instant. Not in the geeky world-domination-daydream kind of way, but in a real, tangible, fire-and-horror-and-corpses kind of way. When Oppenheimer watched the Trinity atomic bomb test on July 16, 1945, he knew he had helped usher in something so frightening as to be almost godlike in its power—hence his quoting Vishnu, supreme god of the Vaishnavism tradition of Hinduism. So, too, had America taken an enormous power upon its shoulders, a responsibility so vast it's unlikely many of us could truly grasp it. Science-fiction writers had been warning of atomic holocaust for some years already, but when their speculation was made reality, the world changed. We stood then on the third stone from the sun, animals still, but now animals with the ability to crack the very stone upon which we stood. Oppenheimer did not need Stan Lee to tell him what wielding such great power meant.

This has become one of the two most clichéd quotations in science fiction. The other is Percy Shelley's "Look upon my works, ye Mighty, and despair."

"THE COSMOS IS ALSO WITHIN US. WE'RE MADE OF STAR STUFF."

—CARL SAGAN

"WE ARE ALL CONNECTED: TO EACH OTHER, BIOLOGICALLY; TO THE EARTH, CHEMICALLY; TO THE REST OF THE UNIVERSE, ATOMICALLY."

—NEIL DEGRASSE TYSON

FAMOUSLY AGNOSTIC, Carl Sagan carried us with him on his search for God. That search extended to the edges of the universe, and on an episodic basis Sagan reported back to us with his results: that we were insignificant, yet magnificent. That human life, and Earth itself, formed a part of the cycle of stellar birth and death. In a way, Sagan almost single-handedly fought off the modern encroachment of creationism, intelligent design, and other religious efforts to downplay science, by offering a competing and equally powerful spiritualism—the conscious awareness of our place in the physical universe. He made us *feel* his excitement and humility at astronomical discoveries; using the latest technologies, he *showed* us the miracles taking place at any given moment, at the limit of our telescopic vision. For any number of geeks and non-geeks, Sagan was the only priest whose catechisms made sense, and his temple—the vault of the heavens itself—became the only church worthy of their worship.

Sagan's iconic catchphrase "billions and billions"—of stars, that is—is another one of those linguistic formulations that fans distilled from several almost-but-not-quite things their hero actually said. Sagan eventually picked up on it and made it so.

"IT'S A NOBLE GOAL THAT SCIENCE SHOULD BE APOLITICAL, ACULTURAL, AND ASOCIAL, BUT IT CAN'T BE, BECAUSE IT'S DONE BY PEOPLE WHO ARE ALL THOSE THINGS."

—MAE JEMISON

"HE WHO BREAKS A THING TO FIND OUT WHAT IT IS, HAS LEFT THE PATH OF WISDOM."

—GANDALF, *THE LORD OF THE RINGS*

THE EXISTENCE OF GEEKDOM is proof that science can never be just science. Geeks are science's *fans*. We love it, celebrate it, grok and cherish it, and are willing to defend it to the death—occasionally with a fervor bordering on zealotry. But this is necessary, as the fans of science have a collective nemesis: the anti-intellectualism so pervasive in much of American society. Given the influence that this anti-intellectualism exerts over education, religion, politics, the media, and more, it's a good thing so many of us are in science's corner. Science could use a friend or two.

At the same time, it's important to pay attention to who, exactly, is befriending it.

In the early 1940s, using victims from their concentration camps, the Nazis began a series of experiments on humans that even today chills the blood. Body parts such as bone and muscle were removed without anesthesia. In chronicling the effects of freezing on the human body, some victims were forced to endure agonizing hours inside tanks of ice water. Thousands of victims were poisoned, gassed, or burned using phosphorous material from incendiary bombs. Those who were not left mutilated and disabled—and many who were—were then murdered so that Nazi scientists could study the experiments' impact on their bodies postmortem. Few dispute the unspeakably barbaric, inhumane nature of these experiments, but as a fait accompli, they nonetheless presented humanity with a dilemma: whether it's ethical to use the data derived from them.

So consider Gandalf's distinction: There is knowledge and there is wisdom. They are in no way mutually exclusive; nor are they the same. Science brings us one; it can bring us the other. If we are attentive.

THERE ARE REASONS TO FEAR SCIENCE. For every valuable advance it gives us—extending and improving human life, providing sufficient food for billions of people, generating energy from wind and water—it has its ugly moments, too. The Tuskeegee syphilis experiments, replicated in Guatemala. Early nuclear weapons testing, which irradiated locations like Bikini Atoll and afflicted the inhabitants with death, miscarriages, and deformities. Early pseudosciences like phrenology and eugenics, which did more to advance bigotry than understanding. Science is a tool like any other, and it can be subverted to serve even the basest human aims. The Large Hadron Collider, however, was not one of these perversions. Much of the concern over its activation was the result of media sensationalism and wild speculation by amateurs: *Could it create a black hole that will consume the entire planet???* Well . . . no. And though many knowledgeable geeks found it hilarious, the public's reaction was both predictable and preventable, given science's history of keeping horrors on the down-low. If scientists want to avoid future hysterias, they're going to need to find better ways of talking with the rest of us. Easier said than done, we know. But come on, scientists, you're supposed to be smart.

The awesome thing about this website is that it contains only one word. The even awesomer thing is that it would do its job just as well with no words at all.

"REALITY IS MERELY AN ILLUSION, ALBEIT A VERY PERSISTENT ONE."

—ALBERT EINSTEIN

T O THINK OUTSIDE THE BOX, one must first forget there *is* a box. Ours is a reality infinitely more complex and downright strange than we realize. Given how persistent such bothers can be, it's easy to forget that our world is not in fact made of 40-hour work weeks, bills to be paid, and lawns to be mowed—though, sure, those things are real—but rather is constructed of miraculously tiny neutrinos passing through our bodies by the billion, galactic clusters on a scale more immense than the human mind can fathom, particles that can exist in two places at once, and seemingly magical universal laws that dictate the movements of invisible atoms and distant stars. The stuff of our world, both on the large scale and the small, comes together to create a cosmos that looks mundane to our unimaginative eyes yet operates as a practically incomprehensibly complex interlocking system of functions. So is our experiential everyday reality the true one, or is the invisible reality of micro- and macroscopic models the true one? The answer, of course, is *yes*.

It's an urban legend that Einstein had a wardrobe filled with multiple copies of the same suit so he wouldn't have to waste mental energy figuring out what to wear. But it's a popular enough legend that Marvel Comics writers decided Bruce Banner was emulating Einstein, and used that as justification for why the Hulk was so frequently depicted wearing purple pants.

"THERE IS NO SPOON."

— THE MATRIX

O F ALL THE PEOPLE who tried desperately to make Neo understand a damn thing that was happening in *The Matrix*, it was the spoon-bending child who got closest, by pointing out that the world is malleable because the world isn't real. A little disheartening to a man invested in the realities of his known world, to be sure, but this little home truth came to Neo at a key moment. We've all been the recipient of one of these; at a time when we're confused and unsure, someone tells us some-

thing that seems not only contradictory to what we want to hear, but unhelpful to the point of non sequitur. On the other hand, just because we don't want to hear something doesn't mean it's not good advice. If even Neo was able to grasp that—*whoa*—surely we can, too.

Inexplicably bending spoons became a visual signifier of supposedly paranormal phenomena during the 1970s boom in ESP studies, thanks to self-declared psychokinetic performer Uri Geller.

"SPOON!"

—THE TICK, *THE TICK*

WELL. APPARENTLY, YOU CAN have it both ways. That, or this is just an example of one innocuous object being given two very different contexts. (Too bad—a Tick-on-Neo fight already feels like one of the most amazing missed opportunities in cinema history.) Strangely, this battle cry has more in common with the quasi-Zen aphorism than would seem immediately apparent: The world in which the Tick lives is mostly imaginary, too—an impenetrable, self-congratulatory headspace. In the real world, the Tick is less likely to be a costumed crime-fighter than he is to be your office's project manager, unable to understand what's really going on but enthusiastic about it nonetheless (and more than happy to take the credit for anything that goes well). Since there's little you can do to get rid of him, maybe seeing him as a "Spoon!"-shouting butt of the joke will at least keep you from boiling over and stapling his hand.

"WE DO NOT FOLLOW MAPS TO BURIED TREASURE, AND X NEVER, EVER MARKS THE SPOT."

—INDIANA JONES, *INDIANA JONES AND THE LAST CRUSADE*

AUTHOR ANDRÉ GIDE ONCE SAID: "Man cannot discover new oceans unless he has the courage to lose sight of the shore." Steven Spielberg may have had Indiana Jones offer the above refutation of archaeological stereotypes to the audience with a wink and a nudge, it nonetheless conveys the truth that worthwhile discoveries can come about in unexpected ways. Sometimes it's just a matter of looking up from our maps long enough to see them. Certainly that is something the good Dr. Jones embodied in a lifetime of daring adventures that he rarely sought but that always managed to find him. Whether he was tracking down Moses's box, Jesus's cup or a space alien's skull, it was always the journey itself that proved far more important than the artifact—both for Indy and for the audience. And that's usually the way it works. Setting out with specific goals and specific ends in mind is great—except when that single-minded focus keeps us from finding real treasure buried just a few degrees off center.

An exercise for the reader: Who would win in a scavenger hunt, 20th century archaeologist Indiana Jones or 51st-century archaeologist River Song?

"IT'S A COOKBOOK!"

—PAT, *THE TWILIGHT ZONE*, "TO SERVE MAN"

WE HAVE A RATHER WISHY-WASHY relationship with our imaginary alien races, don't we? For every serene, benevolent alien species appearing in our skies and offering us something we need—usually the wisdom to avoid nuclear war or environmental catastrophe, or the tools to fight off some other cosmic danger—there are two more that just show up and start shooting or, just as frequently, hide their sinister intentions behind smiles. The disguised reptilioids of *V*; the artificial intelligences of *The Matrix*; and, of course, the hungry Kanamits of "To Serve Man." There's no mystery behind the yin and yang of these fictional advanced races: They are us. Look back through Earth's history and we find that many are the "primitive" people who met an "advanced" society of fellow humans, greeted them in trust, and were betrayed with a shit-eating grin. One can almost hear Geronimo or Sitting Bull: "This is no land treaty. It's a cookbook!" So: a planet full of nonhumans smart enough to trap us and use us as they will? Simple projection of our own guilty anxiety.

Legendary science-fiction editor George Scithers, under the pseudonym "Karl Würf," got permission from *Twilight Zone* episode writer Damon Knight to write and publish a "cookbook for people," titled *To Serve Man*, in 1976.

"WHEN THERE'S NO MORE ROOM IN HELL, THE DEAD WILL WALK THE EARTH."

—PETER, *DAWN OF THE DEAD*

ACTOR KEN FOREE ISSUES this signature utterance in George Romero's 1974 *Dawn of the Dead* as well as the 2004 update by Zack Snyder, and both times it illuminates the fundamental truth that we seek divine rationalizations for those problems we can't understand. So it's not too surprising that this bromide offers the motley survivors of *Dawn* solace from the zombie plague in which they find themselves. Beyond merely explaining the unexplainable, the implication is that those stricken with the undead munchies are paying the price for lives of sin and transgression. After all, they had to be going to hell for a reason. At once, we're absolved of any blame and responsibility. If that sounds insensitive or even incomprehensible, tell it to those who said Hurricane Katrina was God's punishment for homosexuality, or that the Haitian people had it coming when the Earth swallowed up half their country. Blaming victims for their tragedies is the most predictable occurrence in the world; we can count on it with reliable regularity even when it's dead wrong.

It's fascinating that the evolution of zombie tales has followed the same path as the evolution of rational thinking: Early myths present the shambling undead horrors as supernatural, whereas the most recent stories find scientific explanations for the reanimation of dead tissue.

"THE FORCE WILL BE WITH YOU. ALWAYS."

—OBI-WAN KENOBI, *STAR WARS*

WE'RE BORN ALONE, WE DIE ALONE, and we spend our entire lives trying not to be alone. However that need manifests, whether physical companionship or comfort from the divine, it's something Ben Kenobi spoke to when issuing his valediction to Luke Skywalker, and it's something George Lucas understood when creating *Star Wars* in 1977. With the Force, the mystical energy field that serves as the spiritual underpinning of his entire fictional universe—quoth Kenobi, "It surrounds us and penetrates us. It binds the galaxy together"— Lucas created a catch-all upon which audiences religious and irreligious could hang their respective beliefs without shouldering anyone out. Of course, that was before *The Phantom Menace* tried to tell us the Force was parasites in our bloodstream, making it the intergalactic equivalent of ringworm. We didn't take that bit of exposition very happily, did we? No—the Force withstands any such attempts to ground it explicitly in science, because it transcends reason and speaks to something more fundamental about human nature: our desire to hold onto something bigger than ourselves.

In the same breath that *The Phantom Menace* (1999) gave us a gimmick to scientify up the Force, Lucas revealed that these very "midi-chlorians" meant Darth Vader was a virgin birth, just like the story of Jesus. Has there ever been a ballsier attempt to have something both ways?

"COME ALGEBRA, ANATOMY, ASTRONOMY, BIOLOGY, CHEMISTRY, GEOLOGY, GEOMETRY, MATHEMATICS, METEOROLOGY, MINERALOGY, OCEANOGRAPHY, PALEONTOLOGY, PHYSICS, PSYCHOLOGY, SOCIOLOGY, TRIGONOMETRY, AND ZOOLOGY!"

—PETER DICKENSON, *THE FLIGHT OF DRAGONS*

NOTHING KILLS THE (LITERAL) MAGIC of childhood faster than watching an evil wizard ground into dust by the furious recitation of scientific disciplines. This diatribe, uttered by New Yorker inventor-hero Peter, is an act of last resort that both saves his magical allies and locks him out of their world forever. There's no denying it was a clever way to rid oneself of an insurmountable sorcerer, but it sent a clear message about the Pauli Exclusion Principle of fantasy: *Science and magic can't occupy the same space at the same time.* Admittedly, the acceptance and understanding of a scientific universe is a critical part of growing up—try as you might, you ain't gonna summon that salt shaker to you with the Force—but many geeks never stop pining for the days when every broomstick was a lightsaber. Nor should they. Myth, too, holds power in the world. The trick is to remember the element that magic and science have in common: imagination. It's both a world-builder and a problem-solver and, when properly applied, can lead you to triumph over just about anything.

The beloved 1982 cult classic animated film *The Flight of Dragons* was based in part on a children's book of the same name by namesake author Peter Dickinson [sic] as well as on the even more classic adult fantasy novel *The Dragon and the George* by Gordon R. Dickson.

"WHAT POWER WOULD HELL HAVE IF THOSE IMPRISONED HERE WOULD NOT BE ABLE TO DREAM OF HEAVEN?"

—DREAM, AKA MORPHEUS, NEIL GAIMAN'S *SANDMAN*

O UR WOES HAVE LITTLE POWER over us without the knowledge of greener grass on the other side of the hill. The search for a perfect, trouble-free world is an inherent part of human nature—a holdover from our days in the African savanna, dreaming of an oasis over the next rise even as we dreaded the den of predators in the next grove. Heaven and Hell are merely those ideas taken to a logical extreme. Neil Gaiman's king of the dream realm knows this. He recognizes that the darkest things we can imagine are meaningless without something to contrast them against. One need not have faith in a higher power to see this in action: What misery does poverty offer without the knowledge of wealth? How repulsive is ugliness if it cannot be set next to beauty? In some respects, ignorance truly is bliss. Yet look again. If humankind cannot see the possibility of a better world, how can we ever strive to create a better world? Our figurative heavens give power to our hells, but so, too, do our hells inspire us to reach for our heavens.

Hell in *Sandman* is ruled by a Lucifer whose appearance is clearly modeled on David Bowie, thus once again proving our theory that *geeks love David Bowie.*

"KLAATU BARADA NIKTO!"

—HELEN BENSON, *THE DAY THE EARTH STOOD STILL*

"LIVE LONG AND PROSPER."

—SPOCK, *STAR TREK*

"HASTA LA VISTA, BABY."

—T-800, *TERMINATOR 2*

W E GEEKS LOVE OUR CATCHPHRASES. Whether brandishing split-fingered salutes and encouraging one another to "Live long and prosper" or saying see-ya-later in a mock Teutonic accent, there are certain sci-fi bromides imprinted on the geek collective to such a degree that we divine meanings from them both profound and profane. Of these, one of the most interesting is the collection of alien gibberish "Klaatu barada nikto"—deemed "the most famous phrase ever spoken by an extraterrestrial" by critic Frederick S. Clarke—used by the Christ-like alien Klaatu to stay the alloyed hand of his robotic emissary Gort from fulfilling its mission to end humanity. Think of it as the most important safety word of all time. The specificities of its meaning lie shrouded in mystery (and remained so even when Bruce Campbell dispatched the same phrase—to unfortunate results—in *Army of Darkness*), but its portent is easy to see. It serves as an uncomfortable reminder that our destinies are sometimes shaped, if not outright decided, by forces beyond our choice and even, sometimes, our comprehension. We want to know the answers—but sometimes, we don't get to.

"Klaatu" has also been the name of a minor alien in Star Wars, a minor alien in Marvel Comics, and a Canadian prog-rock band.

"HE CHOSE . . . POORLY."

—THE GRAIL KNIGHT, *INDIANA JONES AND THE LAST CRUSADE*

WOULD-BE HOLY GRAIL HUNTER Walter Donovan thought he could identify the Last Supper cup of Jesus Christ by its glory. He was wrong, and the divine power of the Grail destroyed him. The immediate humor of the guardian Grail Knight's dry response comes from our delight in seeing Donovan get his comeuppance—he'd just shot Indy's father, and man, ain't karma a bitch. But the deeper appeal of the quotation is the truth we find in its sincerity. Anyone who thinks the glory of Christ can be equated to earthly riches, finery, luxury—in short, to any kind of expression of egotism—is engaging in utter folly. The whole point of God incarnating as man is humility, as is pointedly expressed in Matthew 25:45: "I tell you the truth," Jesus says, "whatever you did not do for one of the least among you, you did not do for me." In other words: God may be great, but that greatness is found in its very smallness and humanity.

The Holy Grail is one of very few supernatural artifacts of legend to impact modern pop culture twice over, in both a semiserious story (*Indiana Jones and the Last Crusade*, 1989) and an utterly frivolous one (*Monty Python and the Holy Grail*, 1975).

"THERE ARE MORE THINGS IN HEAVEN AND EARTH, HORATIO, THAN ARE DREAMT OF IN YOUR PHILOSOPHY."

—HAMLET

LIKE HAMLET AND HORATIO, many of us are conditioned to view existence in "real world" terms. We comfort ourselves with the idea that reaching the limits of worldly education will prepare us for everything that life will throw at us. In the geek canon, this immortal selection from Shakespeare's immortal play sits comfortably alongside Socrates' "All I know is that I know nothing" and (believe it not) "May the Force be with you" as acknowledgment that, no matter how much we think our education has prepared us, sometimes we simply reach the limits of understanding. It's a realization that the Bard's Danish prince arrived at rather suddenly—(being spurred to vengeance by the spectral image of your dead father does tend to make you question things)—but it's a realization that we'll all likely come to at some point in our lives, though probably not by exactly the same means.

Hamlet has been a nexus of geekery in the past decade—not just the London production starring *Doctor Who*'s David Tennant, but the many references found in the instant-classic comic book series *Y: The Last Man*.

W HAT SOME GEEKS CAN DREAM OF, some others will do. As Americans set their sights on the moon in the late 1960s, a boom in science fiction on the page and on the screen created a feedback loop of the thrill of space travel. The moon landing of 1969 was a scene straight out of *2001: A Space Odyssey*, made real by those who had caught the fever of imagination from generations of dreamers. Unfortunately, imagination and funding don't always go hand in hand, and eventually the plug was pulled on the Apollo program. This plaque is bolted to the stairs of the *Apollo 17* landing module, the last manned mission to another world, and is a bittersweet acknowledgment of the end of an era. It's all the more poignant in light of NASA's decision to shut down the space shuttle program. Having traveled no farther than we did in 1972, another era of human exploration is over, and this plaque might be the last ambassador from Earth any alien sphere will see for a while.

A question with no particular answer: What does it say about our cultural values that a hit movie has been made out of a moon-mission disaster (*Apollo 13*), but not out of any of the successful moon voyages?

"WE'RE ON A MISSION FROM GOD."

—ELWOOD BLUES, *THE BLUES BROTHERS*

CONVICTION. Without it, you got nuthin'. And we're not talking about the sort of conviction that Jake Blues had on his police record. When Jake got out of jail, he was a man adrift: what to do, what to *do*? He could easily have ended up wandering through his days alongside brother Elwood, feeling nothing but vague dissatisfaction until he ran afoul of the law again—but then he was inspired. Inspired through such an abrupt and unexpected epiphany that surely it must be *divine* inspiration: He would raise money to save his old Catholic orphanage by getting his old blues band back together and playing to a sold-out crowd. Okay, so it was an unlikely plan, but it gave Jake a reason to live—a reason larger than himself. That's what makes the difference between a life and an epic life: the ability to envision the big picture and commit to it, to resolve to leave a mark on the world that goes beyond the imprint of pure self-gratification. And that's true whether the god fueling your mission is Jake's God, a secular awareness of the larger cosmos, or something else entirely.

"THIS IS AN IMAGINARY STORY. BUT THEN, AREN'T THEY ALL?"

—ALAN MOORE,
SUPERMAN: WHATEVER HAPPENED TO THE MAN OF TOMORROW?

From the 1950s through the 1980s, DC Comics would occasionally publish Superman stories based on offbeat scenarios that weren't part of the ongoing continuity of the regular monthly serial. The editors distinguished these fun hypothetical tales (President Superman! Superman's bratty kid! Superman and Batman as adopted brothers!) by noting on the cover: "An Imaginary Story"—as opposed to the "real" continuing saga of the familiar Superman. Yet this terminology begs the obvious question, which DC finally allowed postmodern comics pioneer Alan Moore to pose in the introduction to *Superman* #423. Yes, indeed, they are *all* imaginary stories—a fact that can get lost sometimes by the devoted fan of any serial set in a long-running, carefully consistent fictional world. DC, its rival Marvel Comics, the *Star Trek* franchise: all these massive narrative constructs created fans who frequently loved cataloging and cross-referencing the details of the world as much as they loved the characters themselves. That's one big reason why geeks often get so upset at the news that their favorite fictional property is going to be "rebooted" for a new audience. But the thing is, that's precisely how a legend grows and endures—by being retold again and again. Would anyone remember Hercules today if the Greek storyteller who first spun his tale insisted on maintaining creative control? If the fifteenth-century balladeer who sang rhymes about Robin Hood had been able to force all those who came after him to refrain from spinning their own variations, would Maid Marian or Richard the Lionheart have ever shown up? As hard as it may be to look at a long-running quasi-epic and admit, "You know, this was awesome, but I'm bored—let's start over and do it differently," there's probably no better way to take a regular old good story and elevate it to the realm of timeless myth.

VI.
IN THE YEAR 2525

(WISDOM ABOUT THE FUTURE)

"END OF LINE."

—CYLON HYBRID, *BATTLESTAR GALACTICA*;
ALSO, MASTER CONTROL PROGRAM, *TRON*

"RESISTANCE IS FUTILE."

—THE BORG, *STAR TREK: THE NEXT GENERATION*

"UPGRADING
IS COMPULSORY."

—THE CYBERMEN, *DOCTOR WHO*

THERE'S SOMETHING EXISTENTIAL about modern culture's fear of "the Singularity," author Vernor Vinge's name for the moment when technology will have advanced so far that it transforms humanity, or perhaps transcends it, in a way we cannot yet anticipate. That hasn't stopped us from envisioning that posthuman future in stories, and usually we figure it'll be pretty terrible for those of us still confined to meat-sack bodies when the time comes. That's because the mechanized consciousness—which we imagine will approach the world with algorithmic fascism, uttering stark declaratives that allow no dissent—is always terrifying, whether it comes in the form of evil software like *Tron*'s Master Control and *Terminator*'s Skynet or flesh-and-blood entities like *Battlestar Galactica*'s Hybrid and *Star Trek*'s Borg, so cyberneticized as to be unrecognizable as human. But why are we so sure future evolution will produce souls lesser than the ones we have now? Humans are always afraid of anything they see as "the Other." But isn't it likely that new intelligences will look upon us "old" earthlings—so biased, change resistant, and irrational that we don't even need to wait for tomorrow's people to enthusiastically slaughter groups of our fellow humans today—and find us much scarier?

When the Borg debuted on *Star Trek* in 1989, *Doctor Who* fans immediately lamented that they were an improved rip-off of *Who*'s Cybermen, first introduced in 1966. Both spacefaring cyborg races would ultimately be pwned by the badassery of the reimagined *Battlestar Galactica*'s Cylons (2005).

"ANY SUFFICIENTLY ADVANCED TECHNOLOGY IS INDISTINGUISHABLE FROM MAGIC."

—CLARKE'S LAW

SOMEDAY, history will look back and name science-fiction author Arthur C. Clarke one of the twentieth century's most visionary thinkers. Never mind that he invented the concept of the modern satellite communication network back in 1945 (and not just in a work of fiction; he formally proposed it in a technical paper). Clarke's Law posits a truth that ought to remind atheists and believers alike to be humble about their philosophies. If you could go back in time and land a helicopter in front of a crowd of ancient Babylonians, they would think you must be a god or a wizard. This teaches us two things: First, the obvious conclusion that things appearing to be magic aren't truly supernatural but are merely based on knowledge unknown to the viewer. And, second, the too-often-neglected corollary that, at any given point in human history (including right now), a vast amount of knowledge *still is* unknown to us. Clarke's Law sums up the point of his classic *2001* in just eight words—for all the miracles science has uncovered and produced, we're still just infants in the perspective of the cosmos. And the idea that "the ultimate truth of existence" can even be *imagined* by the human mind is hilariously preposterous.

Clarke offered up three laws of futuristic prediction in the 1960s and "70s; it was the third that grabbed the popular imagination and was remembered as "Clarke's Law."

"THE SKY ABOVE THE PORT WAS THE COLOR OF TELEVISION, TUNED TO A DEAD CHANNEL."

—WILLIAM GIBSON, *NEUROMANCER*

TECHNOLOGY is not the warm, inviting thing we've been led to believe; so says William Gibson in the opening line of *Neuromancer*. Our world is blanketed in tech—so much so, we don't notice just how amazing it is. Yet despite these remarkable devices that hold us together, that feed us information, that wire us into something much larger than ourselves, the world can be as empty and ugly and barren of genuine humanity as it has ever been. It's a dead channel, flickering, gray, unclear. So Gibson asks: As we march inexorably forward into our world of circuits and wireless, when do we look back to consider what we're leaving behind? In the world of *Neuromancer*, we don't. It's as bleak  and hopeless as the Black Death or the Great Depression. In the end, technology in and of itself changes nothing. The poor are still poor. The streets are still dangerous. And human beings are still human beings. So we've got to ask the follow-up question: How do we make sure that doesn't happen to us?

William Gibson coined the word *cyberspace* and was a key figure in launching the science-fiction subgenre of cyberpunk. We should not, however, blame him for science fiction fans' corollary practice of adding the word "punk" as a suffix to anything else they've subsequently wanted to dub an exciting subgenre.

"ROADS? WHERE WE'RE GOING, WE DON'T NEED ROADS."

—DOC BROWN, *BACK TO THE FUTURE*

HEARING DOC BROWN'S FAMOUS oh-by-the-way line today, twenty-five years after *Back to the Future*'s release, with nary a flying car or floating skateboard in sight, one can be forgiven for thinking screenwriters Bob Zemeckis and Bob Gale may have missed the mark just slightly when positing their far-flung future world of 2015. However, as Doc shuffles Marty McFly into the newly airborne DeLorean time machine, the import of his words can be seen reverberating through the history of human innovation going as far back as the mind can wander, in our ability to consistently rethink reality and expand the boundaries of the possible. To enact the *paradigm shift*. That phrase, popularized by Thomas Kuhn in the 1960s before it morphed into a clichéd business buzzword, may have withered from extreme overuse in the '80s and '90s, but it remains a potent concept that's put into practice every time we venture off the beaten path for a great advancement that changes the world, whether you're talking about the invention of fire or the cellular phone network. Those flux-capacitor moments aren't as rare as they seem, but they're every bit as profound.

In a making-of documentary of *Back to the Future Part II* (1989), filmmaker Bob Zemeckis deadpanned the facetious "fact" that hoverboards were a real invention being kept from American streets by regulatory red tape. A remarkable number of people believed this.

"I'LL CONTROL-ALT-DELETE YOU!"

—WEIRD AL YANKOVIC

EVERY GEEK KNOWS WEIRD AL—usually more comprehensively than said geek's roommates would prefer. If Al's not turning gangsta rap into a computer-nerd anthem, he's recasting the roughest, toughest hits of balls-out hard rock as bouncy polka melodies. And if the universe is just, Al will live to enjoy the serious critical acclaim he deserves as a creative visionary. It's easy to write off songs like "Eat It" and "I Think I'm a Clone Now" as goofy, juvenile parodies. But when you get right down to it, Al was pioneering the musical trend that would eventually lead to DJ Danger Mouse's *Grey Album* and subsequently to the spinoff literary phenomenon of *Pride and Prejudice and Zombies*. By inserting elements of an unexpected genre into the chart-toppers of another, Al arguably became the first superstar of mash-up culture. To those who argue that such Frankensteined hybrids cheapen the original art, we'd point out that they usually serve to make the original sell *better*. And to those who argue that there's no true creative spirit at work in this kind of endeavor, we would invite them to take a serious stab at doing it themselves first, to find out just how wrong they are.

Why is Weird Al shaking a tambourine in the Hanson brothers' 2010 music video "Thinking 'Bout Somethin'"? We presume it's for the same reason that there was a watermelon in the laboratory in *The Adventures of Buckaroo Banzai across the 8th Dimension*.

"WITHIN A FEW YEARS, A SIMPLE AND INEXPENSIVE DEVICE, READILY CARRIED ABOUT, WILL ENABLE ONE TO RECEIVE ON LAND OR SEA THE PRINCIPAL NEWS, TO HEAR A SPEECH, A LECTURE, A SONG OR PLAY OF A MUSICAL INSTRUMENT, CONVEYED FROM ANY OTHER REGION OF THE GLOBE."

—NIKOLA TESLA

"WITH THE OPENING OF THE FIRST POWER PLANT, INCREDULITY WILL GIVE WAY TO WONDERMENT, AND THIS TO INGRATITUDE, AS EVER BEFORE."

—NIKOLA TESLA

THANKS TO (A) THE WORK of a certain '90s-era hair-metal band, and (b) the Internet's existence providing a forum for large masses of geeks to casually research history, popular culture has rediscovered the awesome genius of Nikola Tesla, the Austrian American who was Thomas Edison's more brilliant but less business-savvy rival. Tesla invented the process for alternating-current electricity, made a host of electromagnetic breakthroughs that made possible today's information age, and, oh yeah, by the way, envisioned the technological future more fully than just about anyone else then or ever—not just the scientific and engineering feats humanity would accomplish, but the social ramifications that would follow in short order. Geek culture has begun to idolize Tesla as the Smart Rebel Underdog Who Was Right in conjunction with demonizing Edison as the Ruthless Monopolist Who Crushed Dissent. And, you know, it's true, but it's also worth asking if our instinctive fetishizing of nerd martyrs isn't a bit counterproductive. When visionary geniuses get marginalized, get relegated to second-dog status beneath Machiavellian power players, we shouldn't *only* identify with their unappreciated minds. We should recognize where and how they failed to build the relationships that might have made things come out differently—and resolve to make that human factor a priority in our own endeavors.

In addition to lending his name to that metal band, Tesla has also appeared in Christopher Priest's novel *The Prestige* (adapted to film with a portrayal by David Bowie) and, more recently, been used as the namesake for a cutting-edge electric-car manufacturer.

"VIDEO GAMES ARE BAD FOR YOU? THAT'S WHAT THEY SAID ABOUT ROCK AND ROLL."

—SHIGERU MIYAMOTO, CREATOR OF MARIO AND *THE LEGEND OF ZELDA*

ROCK AND ROLL isn't always good for you. There's a reason it usually gets paired with sex and drugs. There's nothing wrong with the former if it's consensual and safe, or with the latter if it's legal, but we all know that isn't always the case. Video games have their unpleasant baggage, too, though nothing as cool as sex and drugs—more on the order of repetitive-strain injury and MMORPG-fueled poverty. Thing is, video games are for geekdom what rock and roll was to the post–World War II generation: a kind of coming into our own. We have created a unique entertainment form spawned from unexpected and disparate sources—computer science, film, tabletop gaming, art, fiction—whose appeal reaches far beyond the audience that created it. And like rock and roll, video games have their share of detractors who warn feverishly that they bring doom and destruction. We should hope so. Games are always more fun when stuff blows up.

"FANTASY IS THE IMPOSSIBLE MADE PROBABLE. SCIENCE FICTION IS THE IMPROBABLE MADE POSSIBLE."

—ROD SERLING

W E GEEKS SPEND AN INORDINATE amount of time defining and categorizing the ways in which we retreat to worlds that do not exist. Looked at closely, however, Serling's variation on the distinctions usually drawn between fantasy and science fiction serves to underscore not the differences between genres but, rather, the similarities. In doing so, it ties geek culture together as a community of daydreamers. *Intelligent* daydreamers. Ultimately, we all want to see and experience worlds that are not our own. Our motivations may differ: We want escape; we want to envision what the world could be; we want to explore dreams both possible and impossible. Yet our need to daydream remains the same. Whether it stems from dissatisfaction with our lives or from an impulse to see shades of fantastic in an otherwise mundane world, one thing is clear: We geeks all share an important trait. It's not just that we can imagine—everyone can—it's that we're *not afraid to*.

Serling's *Twilight Zone*, like the magazine *Weird Tales* that presaged it, inhabited a funky storytelling space where the tropes of science fiction, fantasy, and horror swirled around and through one another rather than maintaining rigidity. Over the past decade, geekdom has begun to break down those artificial boundaries once again.

"MY NAME IS TALKING TINA, AND I'M GOING TO KILL YOU."

— *THE TWILIGHT ZONE, "LIVING DOLL"*

IN 1970, ROBOTICIST MASAHIRO MORI coined the term *the Uncanny Valley*—at last putting a name to what generations of children have innately understood: Dolls, masks, mirror images, and other not-quite-fully-human faces can be unbelievably creepy. Many theories surround this response, ranging from an evolutionarily reinforced fear of difference to a Freudian fear of death. So it's not entirely surprising that so many geeks see these fears and raise them by murder—or even scale up to genocide in the form of the android or zombie apocalypse. There is an added dimension to this fear for geeks, however: fear of obsolescence. We eagerly anticipate the posthuman Singularity—which science-fiction writer Ken MacLeod dubbed "the Rapture for nerds"—yet secretly fear that, when it comes, we will be left behind. We fantasize that magic or spiritual manifestations might bring our toys to life . . . and then, finding us useless or a hindrance, those new beings might make toys of us. It wasn't Talking Tina's appearance that most of us found terrifying—it was her superiority to her human master, whose death she orchestrated with implacable efficiency. After all, anything that so closely emulates humanity is likely to contain its own measure of the human urge to dominate and destroy.

Also: clowns. We must never forget to beware clowns.

"IT'S A MAGICAL WORLD, HOBBES, OL' BUDDY . . . LET'S GO EXPLORING!"

—THE FINAL *CALVIN AND HOBBES* STRIP

T HE WORDS ARE SIMPLE and seemingly uplifting, but also heartbreaking. Bill Watterson's *Calvin and Hobbes* was more than a mere comic strip—it was a window into the sometimes carefree, sometimes cynical, and always absurd mind of a kid who was, if we're to be honest with ourselves, a little slice of you and me. Yet, for all its deliciously ironic sensibility, Watterson ended *Calvin and Hobbes* on a note of beauty and hope and vast possibility. That's because he realized childhood never has to end. Not really; not in any lasting way. We grow up and have families and pay bills, yes. But those of us blessed with the heart of a geek never really let go of the excitement of creation and discovery, do we? Watterson saw what even we geeks too often forget: It's a magical world. Let's see what happens next!

Calvin and Hobbes were named after two very old-school geeks: philosophers John Calvin and Thomas Hobbes.

"PEOPLE ASSUME THAT TIME IS A STRICT PROGRESSION OF CAUSE TO EFFECT—BUT, ACTUALLY, FROM A NONLINEAR, NONSUBJECTIVE VIEWPOINT, IT'S MORE LIKE A BIG BALL OF WIBBLY-WOBBLY, TIMEY-WIMEY . . . STUFF."

—THE DOCTOR, *DOCTOR WHO*

A S THE LAST of the Time Lords—an ancient alien race who watched over the proper flow of time across the cosmos—the Doctor has a unique relationship with the endless stream of instant to instant, day to day, year to year. He sees the odd quirks of chronological existence: for instance, that sometimes it's impossible to predict how a seed planted today will blossom and affect life four years hence, or four hundred. That sometimes you can't even be sure the rules of cause and effect *will* point reliably from past to future. That, basically, our perceptions of reality are fragile and open to debate. While the Doctor is a handy fantasy-myth device for exploring such ideas, once we're open to them it's hard not to see them at work in the real world. Was there a massive conspiracy to kill President Kennedy, or did we do such an intense job of speculating about one that we planted the idea in the mass consciousness and made such a thing more likely in the future even as we retroactively inserted it into the history books? Interestingly, *Doctor Who* first premiered the day after Kennedy's assassination. We're sure there's no connection.

Actually, you can still find the occasional used copy of the 1996 exposé *Doctor Who: Who Killed Kennedy?*

"MY GOD—IT'S FULL OF STARS!"

—DAVID BOWMAN, *2001: A SPACE ODYSSEY* (NOVEL)

ONE DAY—PERHAPS—the human race will progress past this mortal coil, transcending the terrestrial and leaping headlong into the unknown next stage. In fact, it already happened once ten years ago. It's right there in Arthur Clarke's history book *2001* (from which director Stanley Kubrick spun a very successful documentary, which you may have seen). In case you missed it on your local news, astronaut David Bowman discovered that a giant obsidian monolith in orbit of Saturn was in fact a gateway to the next stage of our evolution. At that moment, standing at the precipice of human understanding and overlooking the infinite, Bowman sent one final, garbled message back to Earth that attempted to ground what he was seeing in the spiritual and the scientific. But he found that both modes of thought were simply too small to encompass the totality of what he was experiencing. What would you say in that situation? What would any of us say? Maybe one day—if we're *very* lucky—we'll get to find out.

This quote, which plays such a large role in the sequel to *2001*, is—like the Saturn-vs.-Jupiter question (page 64)—an anomalous difference between the novel and film versions of the science-fiction classic. It appears only in the former.

INDEX

INDEX

INDEX

INDEX

INDEX

INDEX

ABOUT THE AUTHORS

STEPHEN H. SEGAL (editor and cowriter) is the Hugo Award-winning senior contributing editor to *Weird Tales*, the world's oldest fantasy/sci-fi/horror magazine, and a staff editor at Quirk Books. His geek portfolio includes work for Tor Books, Viz Media, WQED Pittsburgh, and Carnegie Mellon. A native of Atlantic City, he lives in Philadelphia.

ZAKI HASAN (cowriter) is a professor of communication and media studies whose commentaries on politics and pop culture have been featured at the *Huffington Post*. His regular meditations on geek movies and television can be found at his award-winning blog, zakiscorner.com. A Chicago native, he lives in Northern California.

N.K. JEMISIN (cowriter) is a Hugo and Nebula Award-nominated science fiction and fantasy author whose 2010 novel *The Hundred Thousand Kingdoms* (Orbit Books) has been praised by *Publishers Weekly*, *Library Journal*, *Romantic Times*, and more. A counseling psychologist by day as well as a political blogger, she lives in Brooklyn.

ERIC SAN JUAN (cowriter) is the coauthor of *A Year of Hitchcock*, writer of the indie comics anthology series *Pitched*, and author of Quirk's recent release *Stuff Every Husband Should Know*. He also edits a chain of seven weekly newspapers around his Jersey Shore hometown, and is currently writing a dystopian science fiction novel.

GENEVIEVE VALENTINE (cowriter) is a pop-culture columnist who has contributed to such venues as Tor.com, *Lightspeed*, and *Fantasy Magazine*. Her debut novel, the steampunk circus tale *Mechanique* (Prime Books), was published in spring 2011, and her short fiction has been featured in *The Year's Best Science Fiction & Fantasy*. Her appetite for bad movies is insatiable, a tragedy she tracks on her blog, genevievevalentine.com.

Many thanks to research assistant Ryan Brophy.